The Consultant's Handbook

Other Books By QualTeam

Continuous Improvement: Teams & Tools
    by Robert F. Lynch and Thomas J. Werner

Reengineering Business Processes and People Systems
    by Robert F. Lynch and Thomas J. Werner

Statistical Process Control For Services
    by Dr. Livia C. Lynch

The Consultant's Handbook

Thomas J. Werner

Robert F. Lynch

Published by

QualTeam, Inc.

Ten Piedmont Center, Suite 320
Atlanta, GA 30305
(404) 239-0050

Acknowledgments

We would like to dedicate this book to the internal consultants who have been our colleagues over the years. We admire their courage and commitment in the unique and precarious role of change agent. We know that we have learned at least as much from them as they have from us.

We would like to thank Joanne Sullivan, a friend, colleague, and expert consultant, for her input on all aspects of the topic of consulting. We also wish to thank Dr. Livia Lynch for her advice and commentary on this work. We very much appreciate the artistic expertise of Bob Clark of Studio Grafika. Finally, we are very grateful to Sallie Johnston for her administrative excellence during all phases of this creation.

ISBN 0-9633398-1-8

Table of Contents

Introduction

The Great Questions Of Change

What Is Consulting?

What Makes Consulting Challenging?

Introduction

We constantly struggle with change in our personal and work lives. Some issues of change are of fundamental importance: Can society be better? Can we create peace? Can we save our environment? Others are personal and specific: Can I get my spouse to change an annoying habit or my kid to pick up his room? Can I get a loved one to quit smoking or be less stressed? Many of us share similar desires for change in our personal lives. There are entire industries built around our desires to change our saving habits, exercise habits, eating habits, and time-management habits.

Often the desire to change is poignant in its strength. Many Eastern bloc countries would give anything to be able to change more quickly to capitalism. CEOs trying to turn around corporate dinosaurs would do anything to have the nimble, can-do cultures that they read about.

The question is how to change.

This is where consultants, serving as change agents, come in. Consultants, collaborating with leaders, help people in an organization change.

The Great Questions Of Change

When we are in the midst of a change, we face the great questions about changeability and growth. Can everyone change successfully? Are some people better at changing than others? Can you get better at change through practice? Is a leader essential for organizational change, and what should the leader do? Is a change agent necessary for change? How does a change agent help a successful transition occur? Is there a difference between change that a person initiates and change that is initiated from outside? Where does resistance to change come from? Why does change make us uncomfortable? What's the best way to help someone change? What's the best way to help an organization change? These are questions that are constantly explored by those experiencing change. This book will give the consultant a working knowledge of these issues.

What Is Consulting?

Consulting is *proactively* developing and implementing an organizational development initiative and maximizing its effectiveness, through effective relationships and interventions, following a continuous cycle of steps and using specific skill sets, and being responsible to the organization, the relationships, and the discipline of the approach being implemented. Every aspect of this definition is important.

"Our moral responsibility is not to stop the future, but to shape it...to channel our destiny in humane directions and to ease the trauma of transition."
Alvin Toffler, author

"Proactively" is italicized because it is the most fundamental requirement of effective consulting — consultants must proactively shape their roles, relationships, and interventions to be effective. Clients rarely invite consultants to make them uncomfortable. Most clients are not troubled if the consultant's role is gray, if the consultant's access to them is inadequate, or if the consultant avoids confronting them with difficult issues. Consultants must make the first moves, even with top leaders.

Consulting happens through relationships. There is no significant intervention that consultants can do by themselves. Consider the simple example of a man hiring a personal trainer to help him get into shape. The personal trainer can advise and motivate, but the personal trainer cannot lift the weights or run the miles for him. All positive progress happens through the client's action, in collaboration with the consultant.

The continuous cycle of stages are: Evaluate, Plan, Contract, and Deliver. We will cover this in detail in Chapter 2.

The four fundamental skill sets are listening, planning, contracting, and advising. These basic skills are described in Chapter 3. Planning for change is covered in greater detail in Chapter 5. Contracting is described further in Chapter 6. Advising is covered as part of consulting deliverables in Chapter 7.

The consultant's responsibilities are complex. The consultant must be responsible to the organization, ensuring that all change efforts are in the organization's best interest. The consultant must also respect the confidentialities of his or her consultant-client relationships. At the same time, the consultant must be true to the content of the improvement approach that is being implemented. For example, the consultant must ensure that an implementation of total quality management maintains an emphasis on customer focus, process analysis, data collection, quality tools, and teamwork.

What Makes Consulting Challenging?

There are a number of factors that make the job of the consultant

"All is flux, nothing stands still."

Heraclitus,

Greek philosopher

challenging. The consultant must address these challenges in his or her relationships and interventions. Some of the challenges include the following.

It is very human for participants in a change effort to point to past and current success as a reason not to change: "Why should we do this? We've done well up to now without any of these changes?" The change agent must convince the organization that past performance has absolutely no bearing on the need to change.

Consultants deal with multiple stakeholders with multiple motives. This is commonly referred to as the politics of the organization. Personal motives among stakeholders may range from, "I truly want to change the organization," to, "I don't want to look bad." This is normal; the consultant must navigate through the political and psychological landscape of the organization.

During change, the organization's goals and principles can become ambiguous to the most ardent supporter. Consider these common ambiguous messages in many of today's organizational change efforts:

- "Take risks and be willing to make a mistake, but do it right the first time."
- "We are doing this for long-term benefits, but what results can you point to so far?"
- "We want frequent communication and teamwork, but we don't want you to spend too much time in meetings."
- "We want more consensus decision-making, but we also want you to think for yourself and be quick and decisive."
- "You are the expert in your work and you should decide what works best for you, but we also want to establish consistent best practices."

"A living thing is distinguished from a dead thing by the multiplicity of the changes at any moment taking place in it."
Herbert Spencer, English philosopher

The change agent must make ambiguous issues as clear as possible, and encourage tolerance for the unavoidable ambiguities of change.

Many internal consultants find themselves wishing in retrospect that they could start their implementations over, knowing what they know now. We cannot escape the fact that change involves doing many things for the first time (for the consultant and the client). Consultants must learn how to proceed in spite of imperfect events, openly discussing successful and unsuccessful steps.

Often several change initiatives occur simultaneously, creating pressure on the clients and requiring the consultant to partner with other change agents. It is not uncommon for an organization to implement teams, customer feedback systems, total quality and reengineering, diversity training, new electronic communication systems, and new pay systems more or less simultaneously. Changes in personnel, goals, and business conditions during change efforts also require flexibility and reestablishment of expectations.

Change agents face the individual reactions to change by each member of the organization. The strength of past habits and inertia in the face of change are facts of life. The consultant must face the weight of inertia and the tenacity of old habits with persistence, persuasion, repetition, and training.

Before proceeding with this book, think of a situation in your work or personal life when someone helped you make a successful change. Whether the role was formally labeled or not, that person was your consultant. Analyze the situation and the consulting relationship: What made it work? Why was the change successful? What specific behaviors did your consultant exhibit to assist you with the change? How did you act as the client? By remembering and analyzing that situation, you can probably identify specific success factors for change and for effective consulting. We hope that this book will add to your insights and experiences about helping people change.

1

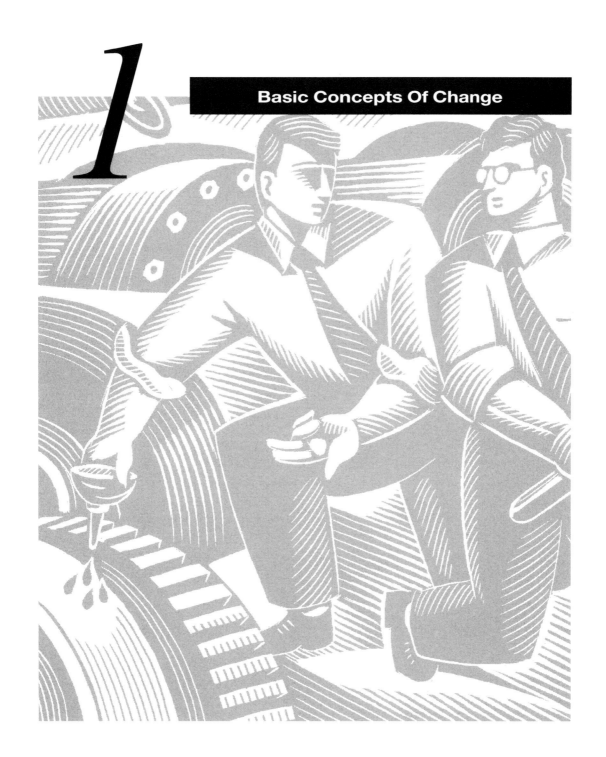

1

Basic Concepts Of Change

It's no secret that the world is going through enormous change. Companies everywhere are restructuring and "right-sizing." No one seems to have enough time. Fundamental social structures like families, education, and health care are under huge stress. Electronic communication is transforming the economy and keeping up with it is a constant challenge. The need for effective change (and effective change agents) has never been greater.

"When our first parents were driven out of Paradise, Adam is believed to have remarked to Eve:
'My dear, we live in an age of transition.'"
W. R. Inge,
Dean of St. Paul's,
London

The purpose of this chapter is to present some fundamental concepts of change and to offer a simple model for change that has implications for the role of the change agent.

Change is one of those things that everyone talks about but most of the talk isn't very helpful. People say, "Get ready for change." But they say it like they say, "Get ready for that big wave," at the beach — you know, you're going to get knocked over but you might as well brace yourself. Heads up! Good luck! I hope it works out. Do your best. Hold your breath.

This book is about helping people change. In your role as a change agent, four fundamental concepts are important to understand:

- *Paradigms* — How you look at things
- *The phases of change* — The predictable pattern underlying your responses to change

11

- *Habits* — How you manage yourself and teach yourself new ways to act
- *Self-care* — What you say to yourself and how you treat yourself when things get tough

Paradigms: How We Look At The World

If you are in the midst of change, your paradigms, or ways of looking at the world, are being challenged. "Paradigm" is from the Greek *paradeigma,* meaning model or pattern — in other words, what we see and understand to be correct. To be effective at change, you have to realize what your old paradigms were and which ones need to change, and you have to be open to changing them. Joel Arthur Barker, in *Future Edge: Discovering the New Paradigms of Success,* has rightly publicized the work of scientific historian Thomas Kuhn on scientific paradigms, who noted that scientific breakthroughs occur when a paradigm shift occurs. Kuhn observed that scientific research follows a steady, gradual pattern of activity punctuated periodically by dramatic surges in new findings. Kuhn pointed out that these surges occur in the wake of breakthrough thinking and during whole new ways of conceptualizing a problem.

Many have noted the importance of how we view things in determining how effective we are. Peter M. Senge, in *The Fifth Discipline: The Art & Practice of the Learning Organization,* notes that "the structures of which we are unaware hold us prisoner." Senge describes the existence of overarching patterns, or systems archetypes, at work in our lives. For example, consider individuals or groups that adjust their behavior in response to delayed feedback. If they are not aware of the delay in the system, they may take more corrective action than needed. Or they may just give up because they can't see any progress. Senge suggests that if we don't look at the "big picture" we will labor unwittingly in circumstances that are actually quite predictable. Noel Tichy and Mary Anne Devanna, in *The Transformational Leader,* describe habitual ways of looking at things that they call "filters" and habitual ways of acting that they call "scripts." For example, we may have a cultural filter that blocks out new ideas about what responsibilities a nonmanagement person can be trusted with. We might have a specific script for dealing with peers or starting a new project. To change, we have to write a new script based on a new vision of the future. (You could add "tapes," the habitual things we say to ourselves. For example, "Nothing bad will happen to us, we're a huge company.") Michael Hammer and James Champy, in *Reengineering the Corporation: A Manifesto for Business Revolution,* describe "rules," the deeply ingrained traditions about how work gets done. For example, we may have a rule that says we must have a hard copy of every invoice that we send. Daryl Conner, in *Managing at the Speed of Change: How Resilient Managers Succeed and Prosper Where Others Fail,* refers to our "assumptions" about the way things are. For example, we may have assumptions about what the organization's structure should look like or how performance should be measured. Decades ago the developers of the Johari Window described the problem of "blind spots," things about me that others can see that I cannot see. For example, I might have a bad habit of arguing with people without really listening to their side, but I don't see it in myself until someone points it out to me. Counseling expert Robert Carkhuff, in *The Art of Helping VI,* describes the first steps of personal change as *exploring* where we are and *understanding* where we want or need to be — in other words, gaining new perspectives, or paradigms. Carkhuff points out that a person does not marshal the energy to change until he or she sees a new way as desirable and the current way as undesirable or unworkable.

The importance of being open to and accepting new paradigms cannot be overemphasized. As Daryl Conner points out, "Accept that you will either pay for getting what you want or you will pay for not getting what you want and the payments may come early or late — but change is expensive, and you will pay... Believe that the status quo is far more expensive than the cost of transition."

The next concept to understand is the set of stages that we go through during change. You may be familiar with Elisabeth Kübler-Ross' five psycho-logical stages experienced by the dying: denial, anger, "bargaining for time," grieving, and acceptance. In *On Death and Dying,* Kübler-Ross noted five stages experienced by terminally ill patients in facing death: first, disbelief and refusal to acknowledge; then rage; then searching for options and second chances; then depression; and finally acceptance. Some, such as Conner, have applied Kübler-Ross' model to people's responses to events other than death, such as responding to a negatively perceived change at work.

The Phases Of Change

Perhaps the simplest and most profound description of personal change is provided by William Bridges in *Transitions: Making Sense of Life's Changes,* who described three phases of change: endings, confusion and distress, and beginnings. These three phases hearken back to historian Arnold

J. Toynbee's observation in *A Study of History* that stated each civilization has encountered a time of trouble and disintegration, followed by a time of withdrawal and return, and finally a time of new energy and direction. Toynbee notes that the basic pattern has applied to ancient as well as modern civilizations, advanced as well as simple, eastern as well as western. Noel Tichy and Stratford Sherman, in *Control Your Destiny or Someone Else Will*, have described Bridges' three phases in the context of a larger model for organizational change being used at General Electric. In the GE model, organizational change happens in three acts. In the first act "Awakening," the organization's confrontation of its need for transformation corresponds to and interacts with individuals' struggles with related personal endings. The need to change and resistance to change are evident. In the second act "Envisioning," the organization creates a motivating vision and mobilizes commitment. Individuals are in a transition period. The new vision provides individuals with a perspective on both endings and new beginnings. In the third act "Rearchitecturing," the organization builds a new social architecture. Correspondingly, individuals embark on new beginnings and learn new scripts for successful behavior.

Endings

Bridges notes that every transition begins with an ending. Those who initiate a change may tend to minimize the importance of ending the old way, as if that would be admitting that the change was a mistake. On the other hand, those who go into change unwillingly may find it hard to admit that a new beginning is at hand — they mournfully focus on the ending of the old way.

"Change is not made without inconvenience, even from worse to better."
Richard Hooker, English theologian

Those forced to change may even be emotionally invested in seeing no good come of the change. The key point is that we have to say good-bye to and mourn the old way, even if the new way is something we want.

The concept of endings explains a lot. You may wonder why people complain even when they get the change they want: "I wish I could have more control over my work — Hey, who's going to tell me what to do?" It's because *we tend to identify ourselves with the circumstances of our lives.* That's the rest of that maxim: "Be careful what you wish for you just might get it...then you'll have to say good-bye to something familiar that you identify as a part of *you* and adjust to something unfamiliar that's not yet a part of *you*." (O.K., the whole maxim is not as catchy.)

The concept of endings also explains why *people generally like to change but they do not like to be changed.* A person who is initiating a change is often prepared to say good-bye to the old way (or already has) and is prepared to embrace a new way of his or her choosing. That person may have already envisioned a new self, one that is connected to the new way. If a person is forced into a change, then he or she must define a new self on someone else's timetable.

Bridges notes that there are several stages within an ending:

Disengagement

In this phase of the ending we are separated from the familiar, thus deprived of familiar ways of knowing ourselves. For example, the loved one is gone or the job no longer exists.

16

"Nothing in

the world lasts

Save eternal change."

Honorat de Bueil ,

Marquis de Racan,

French poet

Disidentification

Most people at some point during a change feel that they are not quite sure who they are anymore. In this phase of the ending, we have to give up former ways of defining ourselves. For example, a recent college graduate in her first full-time job can no longer think of herself as "a college student."

Disenchantment

During this phase of the ending we have to realize that a big part of our old reality was in our heads, not in the situation. The "enchantment" that we held for the previous situation was what we longed for: the flawless, ideal relationship, job, neighborhood, or whatever. To make a successful change, we have to become disenchanted with the old way, but not disillusioned. Disillusioned people reject the earlier case but keep the old enchanted view of, for example, a job or romantic relationship, staying on a perpetual quest for the perfect one and always being disappointed.

Disorientation

In this phase of the ending we lose our sense of direction. We tend to lose interest in old goals and plans. Things that used to be important don't seem so important now. In an ending, we are torn between the desire to keep going and growing, and the impulse to stay and repeat. It is important to let ourselves and others react to endings. *Endings are ordeals because they challenge our sense of who we are.*

The Neutral Zone

After the ending phase, we experience a vague, fuzzy time that Bridges

17

calls "the neutral zone." This phase is a period of confusion and stress because there is a gap in continuity between the old and new. There is a great feeling of emptiness during this phase, but the neutral zone is important because it is only from the perspective of the old way that the new way looks frightening — from any other perspective, it just looks like another chapter of life. In other words, the new job looks intimidating because it's new to *you* — but to everyone else, it's just work!

In the neutral zone we have to take the opportunity to discover what we really want. We have to think of what would be unlived if life just stopped and we didn't begin anew.

Beginning Anew

In this final phase we must embrace the new. We have to stop getting ready and *act.* We have to identify ourselves with the final result of the new beginning. What is it going to feel like when we've actually done whatever it is that we're setting out to do? As Bridges points out, "we have to take things step by step and resist the siren song that tells of some other route where everything is exciting and meaningful."

Habits: How We Learn New Ways Of Acting

The third concept that is essential during change is habit formation, that is, how we learn and how we teach ourselves new routines. As human beings, we learn to act in certain ways under certain circumstances to be successful. When we are successful on some regular basis, our actions become habits and we act competently on a routine basis. When the circumstances change or

"Nothing endures but change."

Heraclitus,

Greek philosopher

when our actions are not successful anymore, we may continue fruitlessly, trying the same action harder or we may simply stop altogether. Obviously, neither of these responses is effective for becoming successful. Instead, we need to learn new ways of acting that can succeed in the new circumstances. We may learn by trial-and-error, by observation, or through someone's coaching.

When we do, our new actions may not be successful at first because we are still learning them. In this case, we need to encounter some shorter-term sense of success, usually in the form of recognition from others, so that we don't return to the old habits or give up. The basics of learning are important here: the more frequent and immediate the recognition from others, the stronger our new ways of acting become. Short-term targets and small improvement steps make this easier. Feedback on our behavior and opportunities to practice are essential.

Self-care: Staying Centered During Change

The final concept for succeeding in change is having ways of staying sane, handling setbacks, and being persistent. As business writer Stratford Sherman points out about today's world: "Global competition demands the best of you. Getting centered has never been more important."

Bridges, in *Transitions: Making the Most of Life's Changes,* offers some ways of taking care of yourself during change:

- Figure out what is actually changing. Don't be the victim of formless fears. For example, the end of a job does not mean that you will never have another one.
- Decide what's really over for you. Whatever is really over for you is an ending and you have to work through the stages of an ending. If technology has changed the way your job is done, then your everyday routines and skills are at an end and you have to face that.
- Identify your continuities and consider your possibilities in a new light (new paradigms!). For example, if you are moving to a new city from a city where you enjoyed many activities and hobbies, your *interest* in those activities is a continuity and can be channeled into opportunities in the new city.
- Experiment a little with change every day. Learn a new piece of software on your computer. Read a different type of magazine. Try a different type of restaurant. Make a plan for yourself about how you will proceed through the phases of change. Remember that even positive changes put you through the phases of change.

Daryl Conner describes *resilience* during change as an important characteristic to develop. As Conner observes them, resilient people are:

- *Positive* — They display a sense of self-assurance based on viewing life as complex but filled with opportunity.
- *Focused* — They have a clear vision of what they want.
- *Flexible* — They respond pliably to uncertainty.
- *Organized* — Although flexible, they develop structured approaches to managing ambiguity.
- *Proactive* — They engage change rather than defend against it.

Knowledge of the power of paradigms, awareness of the phases we go through, skill in changing our habits, and the ability to keep going are essential for successful individual change.

A Model For Change

How should a change agent think about change? The following is a simple but powerful model for change that has strong implications for the role of the change agent.

Our experience of change occurs in four stages: Awareness, Understanding, Implementation, and Change. In the Awareness stage, we must discover why the change is important. In the Understanding stage, we must learn the

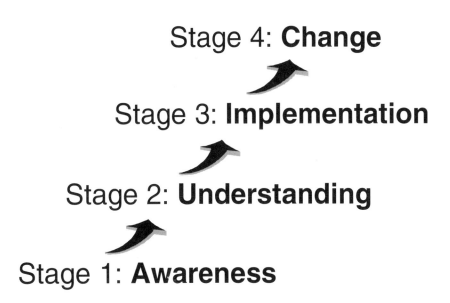

Figure 1.1 The Stages of Change

concepts and skills we need to change successfully. In the Implementation stage, we put the learning into practice and try the new way. In the final Change stage, the change becomes permanent because the new environment (or systems that we have created) support and reward our new habits.

Don't be mislead by the simplicity of the model. The need for all four of the stages is profound. Can you think of times when training happened but people didn't understand why it was needed? Can you think of times when training happened, but the training was never put into practice? Can you think of times when associates of the organization followed a new program because staffers emphasized it, but it never "stuck"? The model explains many simple truths about change that have been discovered through painful experience in unsuccessful change efforts.

The Awareness Stage

In the Awareness stage, we ask, "What's going on? Why should I change? What was wrong with the old way?" We may be excited about the new way, but more likely we feel anxious, defensive, and suspicious. Our self-image is connected to the old way. Human nature and common sense tells us not to throw away familiar routines unnecessarily. Strength of habit keeps us in the old way. Our thoughts might turn to imagined problems with the new way. To change, we must understand the disadvantages of staying with the old way and the benefits of the new way.

"You cannot step twice in the same river."
Heraclitus,
Greek philosopher

We often don't listen to the first calls for change. Sometimes it takes repeated messages. Some of us don't start flossing the first time the dentist mentions it. Some of us don't start saving more the first time we read an article about personal finance. Some companies don't change as fast as they should, nor do some people within a company change as fast as they could. A rule of thumb for change agents is "7 x 7"— a change agent should communicate about a change and why it is important seven times in seven different ways. If you are trying to create awareness about a change in your organization, you might try: 1) a guest speaker, 2) a memo, 3) a video, 4) a breakfast meeting, 5) a voice-mail message, 6) banners, and 7) a letter to associates' homes.

Consider a simple example. Your friend is physically out of shape, and has asked you to help him exercise more. You're a change agent! In the Awareness phase, you must convince your friend of the importance and enjoyment of exercise. Why is exercise worthwhile for him? You might tout its benefits to health, energy, stress management, and appearance. You might point out the dangers of the sedentary life. You might point out that friendships can form among those who exercise together. You might describe that others have overcome barriers of time and fatigue to build exercise into their lives. You might send him articles about exercise, take him to watch people workout, or introduce him to people who exercise regularly. In this stage, you become a cheerleader, a salesperson, and an information-sharer.

Your friend might catch on to your message quickly or it may take a while. If he knows an inactive person with health problems or if he meets a formerly slothful person who is now fit, he may become aware quickly. If he feels comfortable as a couch potato or sees no reward for his trouble, it may take much longer.

The Understanding Stage

In the Understanding stage, we ask, "What do I have to know? How do I do this?" This is the learning stage. Once we become truly aware of the need to change, we are filled with questions. We absorb information about the new way and we begin to practice new skills. Training is the order of the day. Although essential, it is important to note that the typical training class can be an inefficient method of transferring information and competence. In a classic article, Kulik, Jaksa, and Kulik identified the components of effective individualized instruction. The components are: a) a high mastery standard, b) frequent quizzing, c) immediate feedback, and d) regular reviews. Unfortunately, these components are difficult to build into adult training. For adults, training must be interesting, relevant, and dignified. Adults learn from stories, pertinent examples, and if possible, through experiences. A mastery requirement and frequent quizzing can be jarring in adult training situations. This is to say that the change agent must make sure that understanding is really occurring when training is provided.

Returning to our exercise example, once your friend is ready to change, you become a trainer, explainer, and demonstrator. Your friend may need to know which sport is best for him, what clothes and shoes to get, when and how often to exercise, how to avoid injury, how many calories he consumes and burns, the rules and fine points of the new sport, how to meet others who share his new-found interest, and so on. The books, articles, and videos that you shared previously for motivational purposes are now devoured for their informational content. The friend may want to take lessons in the sport and learn its specialized vocabulary and skills.

The Implementation Stage

In the Implementation stage, we must put our new understanding into practice. Often missteps and mistakes occur; support is needed. A truism of training is that, without follow-up, participants usually remember only about 15% of training content and only act on about 15% of that. Though this is shocking at first, if we consider it, it is logical. While participants are in training, their work piles up and the first few days afterward are spent catching up, doing things the way they did them before, only faster. In the meantime, they are gradually forgetting the information and skills they learned. If and when they finally put their learning into practice, they are bound to encounter problems. The real world is a harsh teacher and the learners will probably not be competent at first. Without perceptive coaching and kind words, most participants are likely to return to their pre-training habits.

Thus, implementation by the learner and, if possible, follow-up by a coach are essential for change. The coach may serve as an observer, feedback provider, sounding board, advisor, reviewer of training, and source of encouragement.

In our exercise example, once your friend has developed a basic understanding and competency, you may observe his workout and offer helpful tips. You might suggest a regular schedule of exercise and ask periodically how well he is keeping to the schedule. You may exercise with your friend for a while to offer on-the-spot tips, compliment, suggest different techniques, be a source of comfort during mistakes or injuries, and be a positive factor if his motivation flags. If he stops exercising, you may confront him: "Do you want to do this or not?"

The Change Stage

In the Change stage, systems must be put in place to maintain the new way. A permanent change cannot take place if the environment is set up to be counter to the new behaviors. The new habits must be successful in the environment if they are to remain. Otherwise, change makes the person a cultural deviant.

Returning once more to our exercise example, you might have your friend join a health club or league, subscribe to an exercise magazine, or meet a circle of friends who exercise regularly. You might help your friend develop a schedule of exercise that lets him build it into his life and maintain his new interest permanently. Each of these factors would be part of constructing an environment that rewards exercise and minimizes obstacles to it.

In a constantly changing environment, these stages are continuously experienced. They are not necessarily experienced in the order presented. Your friend might join a health club before understanding how he will use it. He may attempt a sport before understanding how to play it. Or, he may try exercising before really believing that it's worthwhile. However, for the change to be successful, each of the stages must be successfully negotiated.

Four Basic Consulting Services

The model for change suggests four basic services for helping people change.

Communicating

Awareness is achieved through communication. Consider the leader's role in communicating awareness. The leader must be a visionary, describing the new future that awaits those who change. The leader must be empathetic to the struggles of change, but firm in describing the need for it. The leader should never miss an opportunity to give a simple, compelling, and positive message that is relevant to the needs and goals of the listeners.

To help the leader, the change agent must be a communications director, a

Stage	Leaders	Consultant
Awareness	Visionary	Publicist
Understanding	Learner & Trainer	Trainer
Implementation	Doer & Manager	Coach
Change	Builder	Architect

Figure 1.2 Roles by Stage: Leaders and Consultants

publicist, who spreads the word about what the change is and why it is important. In this role, the change agent is forever sending new messages seven times in seven different ways! The change agent may also help the leader form the vision and construct messages about its importance.

Training

Understanding is achieved through training. In the Understanding stage, the leader must be both a learner and a teacher. The associates must see the leader learning along with everyone else. You can't have a learning organization unless everyone is seen in a learning mode. The leader must also be a teacher. The leader must translate his message into the language and concepts of the new way.

In the Understanding stage, the change agent must be a trainer. Traditional classroom training, as well as nontraditional learning experiences such as visits and conferences, are all appropriate. In this stage, the change agent must embrace all of the tools and techniques of the classroom. This is the time for learning materials, exercises, videos, flipcharts, discussion groups, teaching notes, evaluations, and so forth.

Coaching

Implementation requires action, coaching, and management. The leader must make personal changes and manage others to do the same. The leaders must, of course, "walk the talk." Followers watch what leaders do more than they listen to what they say. The leaders must also manage their own change.

The followers will gauge the importance of the change by the enthusiasm and intensity of the leaders' attention to it.

In this stage, the change agent must help, coach, and support. The consultant must leave the classroom behind and join the participants in the "real world" where distractions, disagreements, interruptions, exceptions, emergencies, and conflicting pressures exist. The change agent must observe, problem-solve, encourage, suggest, question, translate, study, debate, sell, and negotiate. He must be both a visible reminder of the change, and a behind-the-scenes helper to those who are actually in the midst of changing.

Designing

The **Change** stage requires that new systems be installed. In this stage, the leader must build new systems that are in concert with the new way. The degree to which systems are changed is perhaps the greatest symbol of the seriousness of the change in the eyes of the organization.

The change agent must be a designer of the new systems and a facilitator of others who participate in the design. With the help of others, the change agent, must analyze current systems, understand how they work, identify the behaviors that drive them, and propose improved systems.

Summary

This chapter has offered some fundamental concepts about change and a model for change that defines roles for leaders and change agents. In the next chapter we will describe consulting as a true process that is capable of being continuously improved.

2

2

The Concept Of Continuous Improvement

The Consulting Cycle

Values, Skills, And Information

Dysfunctional Consulting Cycles

Self Assessment

Consulting As A Process

Being a change agent is something of a strange job. You are not likely to study it in school. The people you would like to help have a tendency to avoid you. Consulting activities are often difficult to describe or observe. Progress is often difficult to measure. How do you get a handle on it? How do you know if you're doing the right thing?

This chapter will present consulting as a process and show you how to use the consulting process model to assess and manage your consulting efforts.

The Concept Of Continuous Improvement

Before looking at consulting as a process, let's review the concept of continuous improvement. In *Continuous Improvement: Teams & Tools,* the authors introduced the PDEI model for continuous improvement. The steps in the cycle are: Promise-Deliver-Evaluate-Improvement (PDEI). These steps are centered around the vision, mission, and principles of the organization.

Promise

The first step in the cycle is to establish the performance promise of the organization and of each team. Each team then defines its work, as well as its partnerships with suppliers and customers, both internal and external. Team actions for the Performance Promise step include defining the team's mission, identifying the products and services of the team, identifying internal and external customers, clarifying customer expectations, identifying competitive benchmarks, and establishing customer and supplier partnerships.

Deliver

The second step in the cycle is to operate the team's delivery system to fulfill the performance promise. Each team should optimize the capability of its delivery system through process streamlining and by eliminating non-value-adding work and waste (including time, talent, money, and material). Team actions for the Deliver step include developing actions plans, following-up on action steps, analyzing and solving problems, and sharing information and recognition.

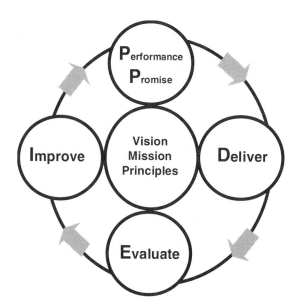

Figure 2.1 The PDEI Continuous Improvement Cycle

"But times do change

and move

continually."

Edmund Spenser,

English poet

Evaluate

The third step in the cycle is to assess the effectiveness of the delivery. Evaluation determines how well the team is performing relative to its performance promise. Evaluation includes data on process performance, output quality, and customer satisfaction. Team actions for the Evaluate step include defining critical product and service characteristics, identifying critical process measures, establishing key business measures, collecting and analyzing performance data, and obtaining measurable customer feedback.

Improve

The fourth step in the cycle is to improve the delivery system. To make and deliver on better and better performance promises, a team must improve the effectiveness and capability of its processes. Effectiveness refers to how well the process transforms inputs into outputs. Improving capability means producing outputs of greater value that satisfy customer requirements more completely. Team actions for the Improve step include identifying improvement goals based on the data, eliminating waste, redundancy, and non-value-adding steps, decreasing cycle time, developing and enhancing team member skills and responsibilities, improving supplier input, testing new ideas, and implementing improvements.

The Consulting Cycle: A Continuously Improving Process

The PDEI Continuous Improvement Cycle can be modified slightly to provide a cycle of consulting steps. The work of a change agent should be viewed as a continuous, cyclical process. The four stages in the consulting process are Evaluate-Plan-Contract-Deliver. The consulting cycle must be centered around the values, skills, and information access of the consultant.

To begin, the change agent assesses the current situation. Based on the assessment, the change agent develops a plan to help make the desired change occur. The change agent contracts with the leader of the client organization, establishing mutual expectations. Once the contract is formed, the change agent provides a set of services, or deliverables, designed to stimulate the change. Next, the effectiveness of the service and its impact on the organization are evaluated, a new plan is devised, re-contracting occurs, and so forth. To be effective, consulting must be a true process. Let's look at the consulting cycle in more detail.

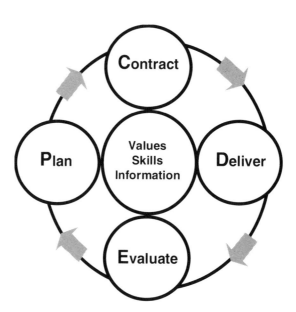

Figure 2.2 The Consulting Cycle

Evaluate

The consultant usually begins in the Evaluation stage, evaluating the effectiveness of the organization and the current situation. How is the organization performing? What do customers think? What are the key business measures? How well is the organization accomplishing its mission? What are the organization's key processes? What measures indicate the capability and operation of those processes? What do the associates think? How effective have past change efforts been? As the consultant delivers services to facilitate change, the effectiveness of the consultant's interventions should also be evaluated. Chapter 4 will examine the Evaluation state in detail.

Plan

"If I know my area of expertise, behave authentically with the client, and tend to and complete the business of each consulting phase, I can legitimately say I have consulted flawlessly."
Peter Block, consultant

In the Planning stage, the change agent should ideally participate in three planning exercises: 1) the "outside-in" analysis of strategic opportunities, 2) the "inside-out" analysis of process capability and performance against specifications, and 3) the organizational analysis of the firm's culture and people systems. In this stage, the change agent should also develop an implementation plan for the specific activities associated with the change interventions. Chapter 5 will present the specifics of the Planning stage.

Contract

Organizational change requires mutual interventions by the leader and the change agent. The leader supplies vision and power; the change agent supplies support and persuasion. In the Contracting stage, the consultant ensures that a win-win agreement with the top client documents these joint obligations. The contract should include the roles, responsibilities, requirements, time, resources, "what is a good job," and "how will we know if it's not working." The Contracting stage is probably the most important and uncomfortable stage in the consulting cycle. Chapter 6 will offer guidelines for contracting.

Deliver

The model for change suggests four basic services, or deliverables, in helping people change. Awareness is achieved through communication. The change agent must be a communications director or publicist, as well as help the leader be a visionary. Understanding is achieved through training. The change agent must be a trainer, and must encourage the leader to be both a teacher and learner. Implementation requires coaching and management. The change agent must help, coach, and support the leader as he or she makes personal changes and manages others to do the same. The Change stage requires that new systems be installed. The change agent must be a designer of new systems and must encourage the leader to build them. Chapter 7 will describe these four basic consulting services.

Values, Skills, And Information

The consulting process must be centered around key beliefs, consulting skills, and solid information. A consultant's decisions about evaluations, plans, contracts, and deliverables are affected by what he or she believes. Each step of the consulting process requires skills which the consultant must develop or manage in others. Of course, as with any other process, the consulting process must be operated in a data-based fashion.

Values

The consulting cycle must be centered around a set of values and habits. Consultants, operating alone or in small groups, facing unique and changing circumstances, must rely on a set of inner directional signals most of the time. Consultants must have rock-solid beliefs in optimism, action, and people as the ultimate solution for a better organization.

Optimism. Change agents simply have to believe that change is possible, and that people can change an organization. Americans in particular are of two minds about the ability of people to change. We seem to be both optimistic and fatalistic about whether people can really change. Movies in which a hero goes through a profound change strike a chord in us (*Rocky* comes to mind). At the same time, we tend to believe in inherent tendencies — it's not uncommon to hear someone say, "He'll never change." We know people (maybe ourselves!) who have tried to exercise, diet, or quit smoking without success, and we know that we have not always kept our new year's resolutions. Nevertheless, in spite of occasional experiences to the contrary, change agents must believe that people can rise above their current circumstances and really change.

Consultants have to remind themselves to be upbeat in the midst of change. Change is a grind and change agents have plenty of reason to be "down" — but they must choose not to be. Clients need optimism, not pessimism, from their change agents during change.

Consultants have to believe that people changing their habits can change an entire organization. We often see the organization as more powerful than the people. Yet if, for example, one by one, people in an organization begin to use words like "input," "output," "customer," "requirement," "measure," "process," "objective," and "team" in the same way, the organization gradually takes on a different feel. If, for instance, every meeting has an agenda and a team action record, reviews performance data, and engenders participation, then the way the organization operates starts to change. If, for example, everyone has similar habits about fact-finding and identifying causes, a new culture begins to be established. If you have ever been in an organization where everyone uses the same personal planner, you have seen a simple example of the power of the widespread adoption of a habit. The effect is powerful when everyone uses the same tools and techniques. Such habits, formed individual by individual, change an organization significantly, such that a newly arrived leader must take them into account. As Benjamin Disraeli said, "I must follow my people, am I not their leader?" In short, change agents must believe in the effect that individuals have in changing the organization.

Part of being optimistic about the future is being dissatisfied with the present. Consultants must evaluate the present in the context of the organization's vision and constantly point out the benefits of the new future. To be optimistic about the future is to be constructively and creatively dissatisfied with the present.

Action. You are only a change agent if you make something change! Change agents have to be action-oriented — change agents have to make things happen. Initiating change requires energy and risk-taking. Change agents have to be assertive. Just like a salesperson, a consultant has to make the "close:" what's the next step, where do we go from here, who's going to do what by when, what are you going to do, what can I do to help? If you read about, write about, or talk about change you may be providing a useful service, but you are not truly a change agent unless you are engaging individuals and teams in the person-to-person, roll-up-your-sleeves work of change.

In that regard, a change agent should be more outcome-oriented than task-oriented. We should avoid getting caught up in tasks that are comfortable and risk-free but do not accomplish the goal.

Consultants should be more outspoken than contemplative. A change agent should be an interactive conversationalist more than an analytical observer. A consultant should be more direct than circumspect. Speaking up should be more valued than making after-the-fact observations. A consultant should be more proactive than cautious. A consultant errs in favor of action and thus makes many imperfect interventions rather than a few perfect ones.

People as the solution. Consultants must believe that change happens through people. Consulting for change must be collaborative because, after all, the client does the changing. Any client can, with a trip to the bookstore or the on-line database, obtain detailed information about TQM, SPC, JIT, high-performance teams, workforce diversity, or whatever the change initiative is. That information is not the change. If that were so, the best change agents would be librarians. The change is people's interaction with the information as they compare it to their own experience and wrestle with its implications for their past and future. People are the change, not the statistics, process maps, or new equipment. A statistician who focuses on the statistics is a statistics *expert*. A statistician who focuses on people's reaction to, and use of statistics, in order to help people accomplish goals through statistics, is a statistics *consultant*. Not every expert is a consultant. In fact, a consultant can be effective without being an expert if he or she can bring expert resources to bear when needed. *The new concepts and tools are what committed, energized people use to put the change into practice.* This is a fundamental point because it means that *relationships* are the fundamental means by which change agents do their work. A change agent who is focused on standard deviations or flowcharts and not focused on relationships will fail. A consultant who looks down on people because they are not using the latest tool or don't know the latest concept has made his or her first mistake.

In that regard, consultants must be more empathetic than judgmental. It's not as easy as it may seem. People sometimes look old-fashioned or unin-formed in light of the future vision. People's struggles with saying good-bye to the old way and embracing the new are sometimes obvious and unflattering to them. Consultants can be tempted to criticize or dismiss them. But consultants must understand the dynamics of change and respect everyone who goes through this very human drama. People under pressure sometimes lash out at the one trying to help. Consultants have to be patient and realize that everyone, including the consultant, does this occasionally. Consulting requires the ability not to take things personally. Consultants must be thick-skinned and internally motivated. They should consider the occasional sarcastic remark or frustrated outburst to be in the job description. Being empathetic also means being open and flexible to the requests, suggestions, and input of the participants. Being stubbornly fixed on doing things one way is obviously counter to an atmosphere of change. Consultants shouldn't fall victim to the irony of being the change agent who won't change.

The belief in people as the authors of change, and in relationships as the consultant's main means of influencing, leads to the importance of being authentic. Peter Block, in *Flawless Consulting,* defines "authentic" in this way: "Authentic behavior means you put into words what you are experiencing with the client as you work." In other words, we speak and behave in a way that is consistent with our thoughts and feelings. Block observed that being authentic is a high-leverage strategy: "We all want to have influence. We want our expertise used. We want to have a feeling of control, perhaps power. The way to gain this control is, in a way, to give it up. Being authentic is to reduce the amount you control and censor your own experience. To censor your own experience is to give other people tremendous power over you. You are letting their reactions determine how you function. The way to have leverage is not to give it away. The way to avoid giving leverage away is to reduce the extent you restrain yourself from acting on your own instincts and perceptions. Acting without restraint is being authentic." Consultants should state simply and clearly what they see happening, what they feel, and what they would like to see happen.

Being authentic also means putting words into action. Don't say one thing but do the opposite — people notice. It is enticingly easy to advocate risk-taking but act cautiously, preach the importance of feedback but not ask for any, or call for directness but complain about people behind their backs. Act like what you advocate.

Confidentiality. To build and maintain the trust in consulting relationships, consultants must maintain their clients' confidentiality. The rules of confidentiality are:

- Don't share anything that the client asks you in advance to keep confidential.
- Don't share a client's negative opinions about others.
- Don't share your unflattering views of a client with others.

Consultants should realize that clients often want anonymity rather than confidentiality. A client may want the consultant to pass along some information or act on it, but without his or her name attached. Consultants should also realize that an individual or team's progress in a change effort cannot be kept confidential. Objective progress is performance data, and performance data is not confidential. Secrets are confidential, facts are not. All participants should understand that the consultant and the leader assess the objective progress of the participants.

Paradoxical values. Sometimes consultants get confused because they find themselves believing two principles that seem contradictory. Some of the consultant's values are, in fact, paradoxical.

Consultants value both directness and persuasiveness. As mentioned above, authenticity is a high-leverage strategy. Consultants value speaking clearly and directly. At the same time, consultants believe in phrasing honest statements in ways that are not only palatable, but convincing. It is better to say, "I see an opportunity for your team," than it is to say "A big weakness of your team is..." To live up to both of these values, consultants have to work at being straightforward, and at using words that validate rather than offend or denigrate.

Consultants value both individuality and teamwork. Organizations change one person at a time, and each individual person has a viewpoint that should be heard. Also, each individual's privacy and dignity has to be respected. At the same time, one of the key values of a change agent is to enhance cooperation and consensus. The consultant tries to create a more cohesive whole. To live up to these values, consultants have to work on both the one-to-one and team level, and be both an individual counselor and an architect of intra-team and inter-team connections.

Consultants value both communication and privacy. Consultants believe in surfacing issues, presenting fresh perspectives, describing others' viewpoints, and in general, knocking down the barriers, blinders, and silos of the organization. At the same time, consultants believe in protecting the confidentiality of individuals who share personal or delicate information. To live up to these beliefs, consultants have to work at "shuttle diplomacy," (at expressing the views of others in a fair and convincing manner), and at maintaining the confidentiality of individual conversations.

Consultants value both risk and survival. The very nature of consulting is based on risk. After all, an effective consultant starts the consulting assignment by speaking honestly to a powerful leader and by exchanging requirements with that person. A good consultant continually resists the temptation to pretend, role-play, and cover up. At the same time, the consultant's obligation to himself or herself, to the change initiative, and to the organization, is to avoid self-destructing, being a failed hero, or causing unnecessary conflict and tension. The consultant's responsibility is to survive and live through the everyday realities of making a change really work. To live up to both of these beliefs, consultants must be honest every day so that directness is not a sudden, deviant event. The consultant must manage the expectations, scope, and objectives of the effort so that success is achievable. Afterall, the consultant is trying to help people do things that are possible to accomplish.

Consultants value both patience and urgency. It has been a truism over the last several years that cultural change in organizations takes five years, ten years, or longer. The need for patience and determination has been well described. At the same time, consultants cannot allow the long-term perspective to make them slow in their interventions. Something should happen every day! Change takes a long time, but time is of the essence. To live up to both of these beliefs, consultants must make long-term plans and then translate them into 90-day, and 180-day, tactical plans. At that point, the consultant contracts with the client to accomplish them, then reports honestly and regularly on the progress.

Consultants value both results and process. Many change efforts have been treated cynically by associates and have failed because they have not been rooted in accomplishing business results. Focusing on business results is the best way to "get on the same wavelength" with the leader and the organization at large. At the same time, consultants look at the ways things get done, the ways teams operate, the ways individuals work, and what people are thinking and feeling. As the consultant becomes engrossed in teambuilding, climate surveys, or process analysis, the line of sight to the customer and the hard numbers of business performance must be maintained. To live up to both of these beliefs, consultants have to keep one eye on how things are done and the other eye on the business results that are produced.

Consultants value both their own perceptions and the views of others. Consultants must be confident in their own perception of what's going on. They should raise concerns or observations simply because they are experiencing them. This is what being authentic means. The consultant must be bold enough to say to himself or herself, "I'm as smart as anyone else, and I don't get this," and then raise the issue out loud. At the same time, the consultant who thinks he or she knows everything, or who fails to respect and obtain the views of others, is bound for failure. The most foolish way to make a mistake is to make one that someone in the organization could have pointed out. The quickest way to create resistance is to act like you know more than the client and to try to change things before understanding what's already going on. To live up to both of these beliefs, consultants must make their own observations, as well as obtain the views of those in the organization.

Consultants value both speaking and listening. Consultants must be able to answer fundamental questions about "what this is," "why we're doing it," and "how it's going so far," quickly, confidently, honestly, and persuasively.

47

The ability to get your point across well in one-to-one, small-group, and large-group situations is a key skill of consulting. At the same time, consulting is about listening, sensing, and diagnosing what's going on. A problem well-defined is half-solved, and the client probably knows what the problem is and maybe even what the solution is! To live up to both of these beliefs, the consultant must focus on listening and, through listening, sense the moments when it is time to speak.

Consultants value both the new and the old. One of the greatest fears of a person in the midst of a change is that it's "change for change's sake." No one wants to feel that one way of doing things is being discarded for another way that's not appreciably better. No one wants to go through the psychic turmoil of leaving one way and embracing another for no reason. For that reason, consultants believe in understanding and appreciating what has been accomplished so far and what currently exists. At the same time, consultants look for improvements, innovations, and breakthroughs. Consultants know that an organization, team, or individual that stands still begins to decay. To live up to both of these beliefs, consultants must study an organization's history, build on what has been learned, and intelligently identify the gap between the current state and the vision of the future.

Consultants believe in supporting people but also in helping them become independent of their support. Consultants are helping agents, and so, to be useful, they must look for ways to help their clients. At the same time, a consultant knows that the client cannot depend permanently on his or her support. The client must accept the responsibility for change and embrace the change independent of the motivation and drive of the change agent. To live up to both of these beliefs, the consultant must make it clear that the ultimate aim is to "work himself or herself out of a job," and make the client independent through coaching.

Consultants feel responsible for change but know that the responsibility is ultimately the client's. Consultants should believe that if they are unable to create excitement, motivation, and competence in the client, they have not done a good job. A consultant should think of himself or herself as an energy source, a can-do person, someone who can "make things happen." A change agent who diffidently and patronizingly says, "It's up to the client, I'm just here to answer questions," is not emotionally geared up to be a change agent. At the same time, changing *is* ultimately up to the client. The obligation to be open to change, take action, and face the future is the client's. To live up to both of these beliefs, the consultant must distinguish between the consultant's obligation to be helpful, persuasive, and assertive and the client's obligation to decide, own, and act.

Skills

The basic interpersonal skills of consulting will be covered in Chapter 3. Those basic consulting skills include contracting, listening, planning, and advising. These skills come into play at different points in the consulting cycle and it is essential that consultants be able to use them effectively and automatically.

With regard to the technical skills of organizational improvement, a study entitled *Voices From The Field* conducted by the Association for Quality and

Participation (AQP) using surveys and focus groups has identified 12 areas of competency for practitioners of quality. They are:

1. *Inspiring change* — Seeing yourself as an innovator, educator, and change agent; demonstrating a strong belief in the importance of quality; and acting as a role model by practicing what is being preached.

2. *Facilitating teams* — Understanding how teams work and knowing how to lead and support them; leading a team through the quality improvement cycle; and establishing a team's vision, mission, and guiding principles.

3. *Training* — Educating and training people in quality and participation values, concepts and methods; developing training materials and providing training as the organization moves toward a team environment; and serving as a coach to quality team leaders.

4. *Process planning and improvement* — Using analytic tools to identify and improve a process; identifying process inputs and suppliers; and collecting and reviewing measurement data on outputs.

5. *Satisfying customers* — Using effective measures to meet and exceed customer expectations; developing measures to gauge customer satisfaction; and identifying customer expectations and establishing a feedback system with them.

6. *Problem solving in groups* — Using methods which help groups reach consensus and solve problems; using the various problem solving tools to generate ideas, reach consensus, and solve problems.

7. *Promoting quality and participation* — Documenting, recognizing, and rewarding the results of quality and continuous improvement efforts;

developing a communications strategy to support quality efforts; and describing quality results in concrete terms.

8. *Designing involvement systems* — Knowing how to design and implement high-performance work systems; implementing self-directed work teams; and optimizing organizational culture and technology to improve quality.

9. *Using statistics* — Using statistical process control methods to monitor and improve processes; developing and using control charts to monitor data; and defining and explaining abnormal variation.

10. *Involving unions* — Enlisting joint union-management support of employee involvement activities; involving union leadership in quality efforts; and organizing a joint structure to provide quality leadership in a unionized workplace.

11. *Assessing quality systems* — Using external resources and measurements; providing information about quality from external sources; and choosing a consultant to help with quality improvement efforts.

12. *Auditing* — Understanding quality assurance terms, definitions, and standards; being familiar with all quality vocabulary; and training the people on the quality audit team.

A consultant must be courageous about testing new skills and err in favor of action, but at the same time know his or her current limits. The consultant should not neglect to use the power of the leader, the expertise of the participants, the wisdom of other internal consultants, the information base of associations, the experiences of other companies, and the guidance of books and articles. The questions are: What skills are called for here? Do I have them?

Can I bring them to bear? Can I sharpen my skills? Who can help me?

Information

At any step in the consulting cycle, the consultant must ask himself or herself what information is needed for an intelligent recommendation. There are some key sources of information.

Data on organizational performance. How has the organization or team performed in the past and how is it performing currently? It is useful to know both the objective data in this area as well as the perceptions of the people involved.

Customer feedback. Customer feedback data is another important source of information. Again, the objective data in this area are important as well as the comparison between what the customers feel about the team's performance and what the team believes are the customers' feelings. There is often a gap.

Climate surveys. Climate surveys are another key source of information. What are the associates' views of the change effort? What are their views of the vision, mission, and principles of the organization? What is their view of the leadership?

Competitive information. Competitive information can help provide a perspective on change initiatives. Are competitors embarked on a similar change? If so, then the change may be necessary simply to stay on par with them. If not, perhaps the change represents a competitive advantage for the organization.

Improvement efforts in other organizations. Thanks to the influence of the Malcolm Baldrige National Quality Award, the willingness of most organizations to share, and the desire of change agents to learn from each other, there are vast amounts of information available about what other organizations are doing in the area of organizational improvement. A local quality association is an excellent first step to access such information.

Dysfunctional Consulting Cycles

The consulting cycle may seem like common sense "Hey, I do that already." Be aware that many consulting efforts fail to "touch all four bases" of the cycle. The following are some common dysfunctional consulting cycles.

Deliver-Evaluate, Deliver-Evaluate

In this version of consulting, delivery is overemphasized. The change agent becomes addicted to finding the deliverable or initiative that the participants will like. The means of evaluation is primarily participants' feedback on how they liked the presentation, consultant, or material. The consultant often judges initiatives by their appeal: "We could do that at our company. Let's try it and see what people think." The deliverables are not grounded in a solid plan or supported by the leaders. The consultant must add planning and contracting to the consulting cycle.

Plan-Deliver-Evaluate, Plan-Deliver-Evaluate

In this version of consulting, contracting is skipped or glossed over.

The consulting usually looks professional because, after all, plan, do, and check is the scientific method. But the missing ingredient is the involvement and commitment of the leader obtained through the contracting step. The change agent mistakenly assumes that the plan and the deliverables have the power to drive the commitment and action of the associates. The consultant does not understand that change requires collaboration between the change agent and the leader. The consultant must add contracting to the consulting cycle.

Plan-Evaluate-Deliver, Plan-Evaluate-Deliver

In this version of the consulting cycle, all of the evaluation is on the plan and the deliverables! The concepts and models in the plan are scrutinized, there is much discussion of organizational theory, and the plan goes through many drafts. This tends to produce enormous pressure on the deliverables when they finally occur, which are often reviewed by the organization like a movie or play "I thought she did a good job of explaining variation." Evaluation of the effect of the initiative on the organization's execution of strategy tends to minimal. The consultant must add contracting and evaluation of organizational performance to the consulting cycle.

Plan-Deliver, Plan-Deliver

In this version of consulting, there is heavy emphasis on planning and on delivering services, but senior managers are not very involved and evaluation is minimal. Change agents can be heard to say things like, "We've been at it for three years and it's going great, but we haven't gotten top management support yet and we still haven't figured out measures." In this situation, change agents' time is often devoted to writing papers, developing plans, sharpening their skills, and designing materials and services. The consultant must add evaluation and contracting to the consulting cycle.

Self Assessment

Answer the questions below to determine the current progress of your consulting in each step of the consulting cycle:

Evaluate

1. What data have you examined to evaluate organizational performance?
2. How will your change initiative affect organizational performance?
3. How will you evaluate the associates' opinions about the organizational initiative and about the organization itself?
4. What data will you track and report on the progress of your implementation?
5. What data will you and your top client look at when planning next steps in the initiative?
6. How will you evaluate your deliverables as a consultant?
7. What charts and record-keeping will you maintain in your consulting role?

Plan

1. How did you decide on your current organizational initiative?
2. How does your initiative relate to real business results?
3. How involved are you in identifying statements of vision, mission, and principles with your top client?
4. How involved are you in strategic planning with your top client?
5. How involved are you in annual planning with your top client?
6. How is the change effort described in the strategic and annual plans of the organization?

7. How aware are you of the levels of support for the change among the key stakeholders of the organization?

8. How involved are you in working with teams on applying your initiative to their objectives and action plans?

9. What plans have you made for your role as a communicator, trainer, coach, and organizational designer?

Contracting

1. Who is your top client?

2. How would you characterize your relationship with the top client?

3. Have you and your top client shared mutual expectations, criteria for success, and requirements of each other? Is this agreement in writing?

4. Have you shared mutual expectations and requirements with each of the units or teams with which you consult? Do all of your clients see you and accept you in the roles of communications director, trainer, coach, and organizational designer?

5. What is the scope of your assignment? Does your assignment apply to the whole organization or does it vary from unit to unit, team to team?

6. What consulting role(s) for yourself have you and your top client agreed to? Communications director? Trainer? Coach? Organizational designer?

7. How proactive versus responsive is your assignment? In other words, do you seek out your clients with a prescribed service or do you wait for them to request your service?

8. What is the nature of your accountability as a consultant? In other words, will it reflect badly on both you and your clients if they fail to make

progress? Or, will lack of progress reflect badly only on the client for not using your services?

9. Is your current contract your first with this client? If not, how many previous change initiatives have you implemented as consultant and client?

10. How would you rate your top client's motivation to proceed? Have you discussed this with your top client?

11. How would you rate your own motivation to proceed? Have you discussed this with your top client?

12. How would you rate the motivation of the organization as a whole to proceed? Have you addressed this in your communications with the organization?

Deliver

1. What is your current organizational initiative? What specific approach are you implementing as part of the initiative (for example, total quality management, process reengineering, or team management)?

2. What types of communication are necessary to create awareness for the change throughout the organization? Do you have a plan to provide that communication? Are the process and resources in place to begin?

3. What training is necessary to create understanding and skill development? Do you have a plan to provide that training? Are the expertise and resources available for the delivery of the training?

4. What coaching follow-up is necessary for application and implementation? Are the resources and schedule set up for the follow-up to occur?

5. What systems will change in conjunction with the changed behavior? Are there plans in place for systems design, process reengineering, or process improvement?

6. Have you developed a self-management plan for managing your time and delivering your services?

Summary

In this chapter we have described consulting as a true process, capable of being operated successfully and continuously improved. In the next chapter, we will examine the basic skills that are prerequisites for effective consulting.

3

The Basic Skills Of Consulting

3

Listening

Planning

Contracting

Advising

The Basic Skills Of Consulting

To be effective, consultants have to master some fundamental skills. Successful consulting requires competency in four basic skill sets: listening, planning, contracting, and advising. To follow the Evaluate-Plan-Contract-Deliver consulting cycle effectively, a consultant should become automatic in using these skills.

The purpose of this chapter is to describe each of the four skill sets in detail and show their importance to the consulting cycle.

Listening includes the skills of active listening and facilitating: prompting, rephrasing, open-ended questioning, effective body language, and empathy. *Planning* requires skills in selecting the best approach, determining key activities, identifying stakeholder support, creating timelines, coordinating implementation details, and tracking and charting progress. *Contracting* skills are those needed for the back-and-forth communication in an honest consultant-client relationship — disclosing concerns, sharing control, being honest about what is possible and what is needed. *Advising* includes the fundamental influencing skills: coaching, persuading, recommending, confronting, and problem-solving.

Listening

No skill is as fundamental to consulting as listening. The consulting process cannot begin until the consultant is accurately listening to the client's perceptions of and feelings about the situation. No client should embark on a project with a consultant if the consultant does not listen and reflect the client's problems and goals back accurately.

Listening is so central to the consulting process that a consultant can sometimes help a client solve a problem simply by listening:

Client: "My team isn't performing the way it should."

Consultant: "That must be frustrating. What do you see as the problem?"

Client: "I think the problem is that we haven't really gelled as a team."

Consultant: "Tell me more about that."

Client: "Well, we've had some new members, we have a couple of members who don't get along with each other, and we've never really had an formal beginning as a team."

Consultant: "So the team hasn't had a chance to establish itself as a team and there are some reasons, both old and new, for that. Is that it?"

Client: "Yes, I think that's the situation."

Consultant: "What do you see as the solution to this?"

Client: "Well, I think we might need to get away for a day or so and talk through what the team should be trying to accomplish."

Consultant: "Are you talking about establishing a team charter in a off-site setting?"

Client: "Yes, I think that would be worthwhile."

Consultant: "What other ideas do you have?"

Client: "Well, we may need some work on the nuts and bolts of being a team — how often are we going to meet, what are our ground rules, and so forth, but I think the off-site session should happen first."

Consultant: "You're saying that some training on team effectiveness may be needed, but the team needs to define its basic mission first."

Client: "Yes."

Consultant: "When do you see the off-site session happening?"

Client: "Within the month."

Consultant: "What can I do to help you?"

Client: "You could facilitate the session. Can you help me put together an outline of what we need to discuss and perhaps some exercises?"

Consultant: "Yes. When can we do that?"

In this example, the consultant used listening skills to help the client define the problem, identify solutions, and establish the consultant's future role.

Listening is required at every stage of the consulting process. Listening is an integral part of relationship building and contracting, interviewing and fact-finding, training and facilitating, defining and analyzing problems, persuasion and negotiation, and handling resistance to change. An exhausted and frustrated consultant is occasionally tempted to scream, "Just shut up and take my advice." This, of course, is impossible! The client must react to the advice, process it, and assimilate it into his or her own experience.

Are you a good listener? You probably feel that you are. Most people consider themselves good listeners. (One can't help but wonder why there is such poor communication if we're all such good listeners!) Most people sharpen their listening skills through communication training or when they have an assignment in which listening is important, such as interviewing job applicants. Nonetheless, listening as a consultant is different in several ways.

First, listening *is* the job. Unlike other roles in which listening helps you coordinate your work with others, listening *is* the work of the consultant. The consultant is constantly sensing the client's reactions to the change effort being implemented. If the listening is off, the very nature of the consulting role is invalidated.

Second, listening as a consultant is more non-directive than "everyday" listening. In other words, consultants don't always know where the conversation is going; they often follow the lead of the client. In everyday listening, we usually know what we are asking about — we listen for specific information and we know when we are finished: "Did everything go O.K. today? What happened with that report? Do you need any help?" Non-directive listening means that the consultant lets the client take the lead in defining the content of the conversation. The consultant is often not sure where the conversation is going or when it is finished.

Third, listening as a consultant is more interpretative than everyday listening. Consultants often "read between the lines." In the midst of change, clients may not be able to or ready to declare their feelings or opinions. Imagine, for example, that a client asks, "What are some of the other teams defining as their performance measures?" The message between the lines may be, "I don't have ideas on measures myself," "I don't want to look bad compared to the others," or "I want to have the same measures that they have."

Fourth, listening as a consultant typically involves responding to strong emotions. Clients who are undergoing change experience powerful feelings of anxiety, anger, or anticipation. The consultant must listen for and respond to those feelings.

Finally, listening as a consultant is targeted toward client action — that is, focused toward what the client can and should do. The consultant's aim is to define the problem or goal, identify what the client can do about it, and determine how he or she can help. Reflecting the client's words back, adding views and interpretations, and determining next steps for the client is the very stuff of consulting.

The basic skills of listening spell the word **PROBE**:

- **P**rompting
- **R**ephrasing
- **O**pen-ended questions
- **B**ody language
- **E**mpathy statements

Let's look at each skill in detail. First, these skills depend on the basic skill of paying attention.

Attending

Listening as a consultant requires simultaneously listening to the client and thinking about the next question. New consultants find themselves "rehearsing" the next question or judging the speaker rather than focusing on what the client is saying. Examples of consultants' thoughts that get in the way of effective listening are:

- "This person is not saying what I want him to say. How am I going to get him to say what I want?"
- "I don't like this person. She is being uncooperative [or nonprogressive, or whatever]."
- "I already know the answer. When he finishes talking, I will just tell him the answer."

As consultants, we must avoid unrealistic pressure to always have the "correct answer" and we must avoid mentally evaluating the client.

To focus on the client's message, ask yourself, "What am I hearing? If the person stopped talking right now, what would I say I have heard?" It also helps to ask yourself, "What am I not hearing?" For example, you might realize that you are not hearing the client say, "I'm looking forward to this change," or "I support the new direction of the organization." Take notes. Note-taking helps you organize your thoughts. Most clients are flattered by note-taking, as long as you make it clear how you will be using your notes.

A good way to maintain attention is to watch the body language of the speaker. Body language should be taken with a grain of salt — a single gesture does not disclose an entire psyche! Nonetheless, Alessandra and Hunsaker, in *Communicating at Work,* suggest that unless we understand nonverbal body language, we are losing as much as 50 percent of the message that is being communicated. The consultant should let the client's movements, gestures, and expressions be part of that person's message. Crossed arms, stiff posture, leaning away, rapid speech, frowning, fidgeting, failure to make eye contact, physical distance, and curt mannerisms all contribute to a message of anxiety or avoidance.

To read between the lines, listen for "high-energy" words, hyperbole, "hinting" questions, and repetition.

"High-energy" Words

"High-energy" words are surprisingly strong words that suggest unusually strong feelings. Some examples are: "That meeting was exhausting," "The vision statement is ludicrous," and "His memo made me furious." "Exhausting," "ludicrous," and "furious" are stronger words than one expects in discussions about meetings, vision statements, and memos. They are "verbal flags" for the listener. The consultant should ask, "What made it exhausting?" "What part in particular is ludicrous?" or "What exactly did he say?"

Hyperbole

Hyperbole is the use of exaggeration or extravagant superlatives. Some examples are: "Those numbers are the worst I've ever seen in my life," "The team I have now is absolutely the least motivated I've ever had," "I've never been so confused in my life," and "This has absolutely nothing to do with the real world." As consultants, of course, we want to probe any topic that our client feels is the "most," "least," "best," or "worst" anything.

"Hinting" Questions

"Hinting" questions are questions that point to another message "below the surface." "How long does this usually take?" may hint at the client's concern that the project will miss its deadlines. "How have some of the other teams handled arguments?" might hint at the client's frustration over recent arguments. "Do you feel that every team has to own a process to be considered a team?" may be a way of saying, "I don't know what process my team owns."

Repetition

Listen for repetition. If the client returns to a previous topic, the consultant should explore that topic in greater depth. Repeating a question or opinion is often a client's way of saying, "This is the most important thing to me." Imagine, for example, that a client were to say, "Going back to the training again, how long is the team skills class?" The consultant might respond, "The team skills class is three days long. Let's talk more about the training. How do you feel about your team devoting three days to the class?"

Prompting

Prompting is the use of short, non-directive phrases that encourage the speaker to continue and elaborate. Examples are: "Tell me more about that," "Go on," "I see," "How so?" "Yes," and "Um-hmm." Prompts may be either declarative phrases or short questions. Repeating a key word, or rephrasing a statement in the form of a question also serves as a prompt. For example, if a client says, "My customers have become hypersensitive lately," the consultant might simply respond, "Hypersensitive?" With prompts, the listener encourages the speaker to build on earlier comments without steering or interrupting.

Rephrasing

Rephrasing, also called paraphrasing, is saying back to the speaker what you thought the person really meant for confirmation or clarification. Examples are: "What I hear you saying is...," "What you're saying is...," "In other words...," and "It sounds like you're saying that..."

The premise of rephrasing is that a spoken statement is like the tip of an iceberg — just as only about 10% of an iceberg is visible above water, so only a small percent of our thoughts and feelings are expressed in a given comment. Below the surface, the client may have feelings and opinions that are difficult to put into words. The client may be uncomfortable with the topic, or may not realize that his or her spoken words have not conveyed the full message. For example, a consultant can take his client's statement, "That meeting on Friday should be really interesting," a variety of ways: Is the client being sarcastic? Is the client simply being enthusiastic? Is the client being purposely mysterious? To explore further, the listener could use a prompt: "Tell me more about that." Or, an open-ended question: "What do you mean?" Or, the listener could simply rephrase the statement: "You're saying the meeting on Friday should be an eye-opener."

In rephrasing, the listener, using the speaker's body language and the context of the discussion, senses what the speaker really means and checks it out: "What I hear you saying is that the meeting will be unpleasant." The speaker did not say this directly, but he or she will most likely confirm, "Yes, that's right." Or clarify, "No, no, I think it will be intriguing. Have you seen the agenda?" Either confirmation or clarification provides additional information to the listener. In that sense, rephrasing as a listening technique is foolproof, unless it is overused.

Recent graduates of communication seminars sometimes irritate us by overusing rephrasing (Speaker: "I'll be back in a minute." Listener: "What you're saying is that you'll be right back."). This, of course, is inappropriate. Rephrasing should be used only when the message is important or ambiguous, or when you want to show that you are following the discussion.

Rephrasing is particularly important as a response to resistance or hostility. Imagine, for example, that a client says impatiently, "I'm tired of all this. This is taking much more time than you said it would." The consultant might respond by rephrasing, "What you're saying is that this change we're going through is hard and that I underestimated how much work it would be." Rephrasing diffuses emotional reactions by clarifying rather than denying, or arguing, with the other person's viewpoint.

A variation on rephrasing might be called "focused rephrasing," in which the listener offers the speaker two alternative restatements and asks for confirmation of one: "Are you saying that this survey will work here, or are you saying that we should look for another one?"

Although all of the above rephrasing openers are appropriate, a rephrasing statement that starts with "I" ("What I'm hearing you say is...") puts the appropriate ownership for the statement on the listener. It correctly attributes the content of the rephrasing statement to the listener's interpretation rather than to the speaker.

Open-ended Questions

Consultants emphasize the use of open-ended questions. Open-ended questions are questions that cannot easily be answered "yes" or "no." Open-ended questions invite a stronger answer from the speaker than close-ended questions. Open-ended questions begin with who, what, when, where, why, and how. Examples of open-ended questions are:

- "What can we do to improve?"
- "What are some things that you feel are going well?"
- "What are the things that you wish were going differently?"
- "How do you think the organization is responding to the new change?"

Close-ended questions can be answered "yes" or "no." It's certainly easy enough to distinguish between open- and close-ended questions. It is important, and not quite so easy, to use more open-ended than close-ended questions when consulting. In everyday business conversations, we tend to use close-ended questions: "Did everything run O.K. yesterday? Any problems?" The same is true with our social conversations: "Did you have a good weekend? Did you do anything exciting?" Our work-related questions tend to be close-ended because we know what we want to ask and we want to be efficient. Our social questions tend to be close-ended so as not to burden the speaker — the close-ended format lets the speaker elaborate only if desired. In a consulting situation, a client may be unlikely to elaborate with close-ended questions (Consultant: "Are you ready for this change?" Client: "Yes." Consultant: "Do you see any problems?" Client: "No."). The client is bound to have thoughts and feelings about the change, and open-ended questions: "How ready do you feel for this change? What's your biggest concern about the change so far?"

may encourage the client to elaborate. Consultants should make open-ended questions a habit.

If you are skilled at open-ended questions, ask "game-changing" open-ended questions. Game-changing open-ended questions do not necessarily flow from the current train of the conversation. They focus on the energy and direction of the conversation. Socially, we may avoid asking such "blunt" questions, but consultants must ask well-timed, direct open-ended questions:

- "What part do you play in this problem?"
- "What is your biggest worry in the business right now?"
- "How can this change effort help?"
- "What aspect of your style will you change in this effort?"
- "If you could wave a magic wand and change any one thing, what would it be?"

Close-ended Questions

Close-ended questions play a role in the skill repertoire of the consultant. Close-ended questions are used for closing, that is, establishing commitments about decisions and action:

- "Do you think you can get that done by Friday?"
- "Do we agree that this project plan is the way we should proceed?"
- "Do you feel that the organization can survive if it continues on its same course without changing?"

Body Language

Effective listeners show with their bodies that they are listening. Here are the basics.

Eye Contact

Good listeners maintain steady eye contact, without staring or excessive blinking. Eye contact is the fundamental "connector" between people; difficulty in making eye contact is usually a signal of discomfort.

Expressive Face And Occasional Nodding

As listeners, our faces should mirror the content of the speaker's message. If the speaker expresses enthusiasm, we should smile appreciatively. If the speaker describes frustration or disappointment, our faces should show concern. A deadpan, "poker-face" style isn't an asset to active listening. Occasional nodding indicates that we are following the conversation. Continuous nodding can appear condescending or indiscriminate. In social situations we nod often to show appreciation and general acceptance. At work, however, continuous nodding risks expressing agreement to something you disagree with. Wait until you really understand or agree before nodding.

Open, Nondefensive, Nonthreatening Stance

Physically, we should neither intimidate nor cower. We should not crowd the speaker, slouch, gaze downward, nor maintain an arms-crossed, closed-off stance. We should stand, or sit, with arms open and back straight. It is best to match the body language of the speaker, leaning forward as that person does, standing or sitting as that person does, and so forth.

"For good and evil,

man is a free creative

spirit. This produces

the very queer world

we live in, a world in

continuous creation

and therefore

continuous change

and insecurity."

Joyce Cary,

British novelist

Lean Forward And Square The Shoulders

Effective listeners face the speaker directly and lean slightly forward, indicating interest and attention. Turning only one's head to the speaker and slumping back in one's chair show the opposite.

Silence

Silence is a type of nonverbal prompt. A silent count from one to six is usually a sufficient period of silence to prompt the speaker to continue. Silence is a useful prompt because all of us tend to be uncomfortable with silence and fill it with conversation. Consultants must, of course, avoid filling the silence with their own speaking.

Empathy Statements

Empathy is being able to identify with another human being's feelings and experiences. Empathy is the ability to relate to another's experiences even if we haven't lived that experience ourselves. An empathy statement is a response to the emotional content of a speaker's comments. A speaker is unlikely to continue after expressing an emotion if the listener does not react in an understanding way. Openers for empathetic statements are:

- "I can see how you would feel..."
- "In that situation I know I would feel..."
- "It must feel..."

Empathy must be accurate. Falsely-stated empathy produces the opposite of the desired effect. It helps to put a feeling word in the empathy statement: "I can see how you would feel frustrated." A way of ensuring the accuracy of your empathy is to connect the feeling to the content of the message:

- "You feel discouraged because the team isn't responding."
- "You feel frustrated because we are not making faster progress."
- "You feel annoyed because you feel this material isn't relevant to your business."

Empathy should be distinguished from sympathy. Sympathy is expressing a shared feeling with the speaker. If the client states a wish that the company's products be the best in the world, the consultant may sincerely sympathize. If the client expresses a hope that the change effort does not become a "flavor of the month," the consultant can genuinely express a shared feeling. Openers for sympathy statements are:

- "I share that feeling."
- "I feel the same way about that."

Perhaps the most profound sympathy occurs when an internal consultant and client share reminiscent feelings about the organization's old ways. As the client says good-bye to that former way of life, the internal consultant may be able to sympathize perfectly with the grief and confusion of leaving behind a culture that both thought might last forever.

Connecting The Listening Skills

The listening skills are effective when combined in a sequence. A useful combination is: an open-ended question (often a game-changing question that sets a direction), followed by a prompt for elaboration, followed by rephrasing for understanding, followed by an empathy statement (if a feeling has been expressed), followed by a connecting phrase (such as "Let me ask you this..."), followed by a new open-ended question which either explores the previous content or sets a new direction. For example:

Consultant: "If you could change one thing around here, what would it be?" *(open-ended question)*

Client: "I wish we had better communication."

Consultant: "Tell me more about that." *(prompt)*

Client: "I think sometimes the right hand doesn't know what the left hand is doing."

Consultant: "What I hear you saying is that there are communication gaps between some of the teams." *(rephrase)*

Client: "That's right."

Consultant: "I can see how that would make work difficult sometimes." *(empathy).* "Let me ask you this..." *(connecting phrase)* "What's an example of a situation where poor communication was evident?" *(open-ended question)*

Client: "Well, my operations team approached one of our external customers for feedback. It turns out that a sales team and special project team had already approached them, asking the same thing. It was embarrassing. Why didn't we know that was happening?"

Consultant: "Tell me about the other teams." *(prompt)*

Client: "I guess the sales team believes that it should be the group that communicates with the customer. The special project team is trying to get feedback from all major customers on our products and services."

Consultant: "In other words, the sales team may think that there's no reason for you to approach the customer, believing it's the main contact. And the special project team is independently talking to all customers." *(rephrase)*

Client: "That's right."

Consultant: "And you feel embarrassed in front of the customer because you look like you don't know what's happening in the organization." *(empathy)*

Client: "Yes, it's embarrassing. And it's frustrating because it seems like we're duplicating each other's work."

Consultant: "Let me ask you this..." *(connecting statement)* "Why do you suppose this is happening? *(open-ended question)*

Client: "I don't think there are any communication links among the different teams."

Consultant: "Communication links?" *(prompt)*

Client: "There's nothing set up where each team would hear about what the others are doing."

Consultant: "You're saying there is no systematic communication and no routine sharing of information?" *(rephrase)*

Client: "Yes."

Consultant: "Do you see that as the cause of the problem?" *(close-ended question)*

Client: "Yes, I do."

Consultant: "What do you see as the solution?" *(open-ended question)*

In the above example, the consultant combined the basic skills of listening into a natural sequence to help the client diagnose a problem and determine a course of action.

Planning

Planning skills include being able to: 1) construct a process model of the business, 2) select an approach, such as total quality management, continuous improvement, or process reengineering, 3) facilitate "outside-in" planning, "inside-out" planning, and organizational planning, 4) describe a clear case for action, 5) construct a planning matrix that shows who owns, participates, and assists at each implementation step, 6) define detailed plans and milestones to measure effectiveness, and 7) describe the business relevance of the change effort. See Chapter 2 for the specifics on these skills.

Business Relevance

Describing the business relevance means being able to explain the impact of your process to your top client and all of the participants. Philosophically, what do you want people to believe? Conceptually, what are the key ideas and new paradigms? Strategically, how will the change help against the competition? Operationally, how will it affect day-to-day activities? Behaviorally, will people actually be doing differently? Financially, how will it help the organization?

Contracting

Contracting is the formalization of a true, reciprocal relationship between the client and consultant. *There are virtually no interventions that a change agent can make without the cooperation of the client.* In addition to helping the client, the consultant must *have* the help of the client. Contracting is the verbalization of the back-and-forth interaction necessary for successful change.

A consultant who is used to listening may find contracting a bit unsettling.

Contracting requires the consultant to tell as well as listen. The consultant must "confess" potential weaknesses in the plan. The consultant must stand up for what he or she believes is needed from the client to get the job done. Some of these needs are likely to be concrete, such as commitment of resources and time. Other requirements of the client are likely to be behaviors, such as full participation in activities, meeting regularly with the consultant, and exchanging feedback with the consultant. Others are likely to be emotional or psychological, such as risking temporarily lower performance, accepting that some interventions will be imperfect, and tolerating the ambiguities of change.

Contracting establishes the consulting relationship, both practically and symbolically. It sets the tone for a relationship that is different from others at work. It requires honesty and openness on the part of the consultant as well as the client. Failure to contract effectively shows resistance on the part of the consultant! Contracting requires several key skills: initiation, direct responding, direct questioning, surfacing problems, and the ability to handle conflict.

Initiation

The consultant must be able to initiate the contracting discussion. "I'd like to meet with you to discuss our roles in this effort so that we're sure that it's set up to succeed..." *There are no cues in the work world for contracting.* No one will complain if you do not establish clear expectations upfront. Most senior managers expect to give you their requirements, not agree to your requirements. The office trappings and body language of a senior manager do not invite mutual expectation-setting and relationship-building. Many work relationships are less specific than consultant-client relationships. Working together on projects often has a "we'll-work-it-out-as-we-go-along" feel, and many managers become comfortable with minimal specificity. The consultant must proactively initiate contracting even if there are signals from the client that it would be acceptable, even desirable, not to.

Direct Responding

The consultant must expect and be able to answer direct questions, such as:

- "What is a good job?"
- "What will it take for this to work?"
- "How will we know if it's not working?"

Sometimes vague phrases are the openings for direct responding. "Anything else you need from me?" "How do you see this working?" "How do you plan to proceed with this?" and "Keep me up to speed on what you're doing" — are all cues for direct responses related to contracting. Opening phrases for direct responding are:

- "Let me tell you what I see as the ingredients for success."
- "Here's how I would like to work."
- "I think this will take commitments from both of us, such as..."

Direct Questioning

The consultant must be able to ask direct questions of the top client, such as:

- "How will we impact your behavior as well?"
- "What systems do you see yourself changing?"

- "Can you meet with me once a week to go over the progress?"
- "What's your biggest concern with this?"

Surfacing Problems

The consultant must be able to surface problems, both in the consultant-client relationship and in the change effort itself. Problems not dealt with do not go away. On the contrary, disagreements lead to growth in the relationship. The consultant must be able to give and receive feedback. The consultant must be skilled at raising problems:

- "There's something I want to bring up and check out with you."
- "I sense that you're concerned that I'm spending too much time attending team meetings. Is that a concern of yours?"
- "I'm picking up some tension on your team when I attend your team meetings. I was wondering if you're picking up anything like that."

The consultant must also be skilled at giving the client easy opportunities to give feedback:

- "I'd like to make sure we're still on the same wavelength. What could I be doing that I'm not doing now?"

Ability To Handle Conflict

Every consultant will, sooner or later, get into a heated disagreement with his or her client. Every consultant will receive negative feedback. Every consultant will hear the approach he or she is advocating be denigrated. Every consultant will have to say, and hear, things that he or she would prefer not to. Consultants must be emotionally prepared for these events. These are moments of truth. Handling these moments with maturity and grace will strengthen the consultant-client relationship and energize the change effort.

The ability to survive an argument is a mark of any successful relationship. The ability to exchange personal feedback without defensiveness or argument is central to honest communication.

Advising

While listening focuses on the speaker's opinions and feelings and contracting establishes reciprocal requirements, advising is inserting the consultant's influence into the client's situation.

The specific skills of advising are: recommending, coaching, persuading, confronting, and solving. Recommending is offering suggestions. Coaching includes explaining, sharing observations, and giving developmental feedback. Persuading is describing the features and benefits of a recommendation, and includes negotiating the specifics of implementation. Confronting involves facing resistance, surfacing conflicts, and expressing disagreement. Solving involves using problem-solving models and techniques to analyze and address client problems.

Recommending

How can consultants offer suggestions without being experts in the client's business? Rather than looking only through the client's eyes, consultants also look at the client's situation from other perspectives. Consultants use conceptual models, past experiences, data, problem-solving tools, and implementation plans to guide their analyses and recommendations. This combination of the client's firsthand experience and the consultant's outside perspective is the classic consultative collaboration.

Conceptual Models

A consultant uses conceptual models to provide insight into a situation and provide a recommendation. Conceptual models serve as "lenses" through which to observe a client's situation. For example, to identify a process suitable for process improvement, a consultant might use a process-selection model that rates processes as High or Low Importance, (to the customer and the company), and High or Low Ability to Influence, (by the team). This simple model adds order and logic to the confusing question of, "What do we work on?"

In addition to using conceptual models, a consultant may have had a similar consulting experience whose solution can be transferred to a new situation. For example, if the consultant has had specific experience in working with teams that are geographically dispersed, those experiences may be transferred and tailored to a new long-distance team.

The consultant may collect new data or analyze existing data in a new way to gain a new view of the situation. For example, the consultant may look at process data in time series, categorize defects by frequency, or collect customer feedback data to shed light on the situation. The consultant may also compare such data with outside benchmarks to provide useful perspectives. (Of course, training the client in the use of such tools would become part of the consultant's deliverable.)

The consultant may use a variety of problem-solving tools to address a problem. For example, the consultant may use a fishbone diagram to organize the possible causes of the problem, or an affinity diagram to identify commonalities among many facts. The value added by the consultant may be in using a tool that has not been used, facilitating client participation in applying the tool, or providing a fresh perspective.

Finally, a consultant may rely on the implementation plan of the change effort as a guide for advice. If a plan has been developed, a large part of the help to the client is in "following the steps in the plan." For example, the consultant may offer suggestions in the context of the set of steps that have been defined in the change plan.

Managers, consultants, and professors have developed thousands of conceptual models to illustrate the dynamics of successful organizational functioning. Every book on the business book shelves contains at least one model as its basis.

Some models that are "tried and true," and absolutely essential for effective organizational consulting, are the following:

Force-field analysis. Force-field analysis assumes that in any endeavor there are driving forces that propel the endeavor toward successful completion and restraining forces that inhibit progress. Force-field analysis identifies all existing forces, determines whether they are drivers or restrainers, and draws them in opposition. This allows the consultant and client to observe whether "the wind is at our backs or in our faces." Discussion can then focus on how to strengthen the drivers and neutralize or overcome the restrainers.

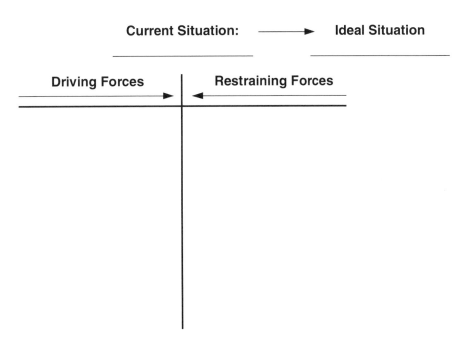

Figure 3.1 Force-field Analysis

Gap analysis. Gap analysis identifies the current state and desired state in order to delineate the gap between the two. Gap analysis is a powerful tool, but its use requires defining what is really happening today and what we would like to happen in the future. The size of the gap between the current and future states lets the user plan where to start and how to proceed.

Process models. The process approach was well described in the aptly named *Harvard Business Review* article, "Staple Yourself to an Invoice," by Benson P. Shapiro, V. K. Rangan, and J. J. Sviokla. To use this extremely powerful model, you must identify a process, that is, a repeatable set of activities that transforms inputs into outputs, adding value. The fundamental questions required by the process model create a blueprint of the process. What are the inputs to the process? Who are the suppliers of the inputs? What are the outputs? Who are the customers, or receivers, of the outputs? What are the customers' requirements? How is the performance of the process measured? How is the condition of the output measured? What information about process performance and product quality is fed back to the operators of the process? What are the steps in the process? Where are the hand-offs among functions, or groups, that touch the process? Who is the process owner? As suggested in "Staple Yourself to an Invoice," the consultant can indeed pretend to be the throughput and look for repeating loops, delays, bottlenecks, unnecessary moves or storages, unnecessary inspections or sign-offs, hand-offs across team boundaries, and so forth.

Problem-solving models. Every consultant should be able to apply a problem-solving model on the spot to a client's problem. There are many problem-solving models — most of them are more similar than different. In *Continuous Improvement: Teams & Tools,* we recommend the following model: 1) *Define* the problem, 2) What are the *Facts?* 3) What are the suspected *Causes?* 4) What data would *Verify* the true causes? 5) What are the *Alternatives* for removing the causes? 6) What is the best *Solution?* and 7) What is the *Action Plan* for implementing the solution?

Organizational or teambuilding models. A variety of organizational and teambuilding models can be applied to organize observations and assess current status. The following models are particularly useful:

The Stages of Change. The stages of change — Awareness, Understanding, Implementation, and Change — are a useful model for assessing a client's progress (see Figure 1.1, Chapter 1). Does the client organization need to increase its awareness, that is, discover why a change is necessary? If so, the consultant must play the role of communications director and help the leader of the organization act as a visionary. Does the organization need to increase its understanding, that is, learn skills and concepts about how to change? If so, the consultant must play the role of trainer and help the leader be both a teacher and learner. Does the organization need to implement action plans for change, that is, put its awareness and understanding into practice? If so, the consultant should play the role of coach and help the leader make both personal changes and manage others' action plans. Does the organization need to change systems so that the changes are supported and reinforced? If so, the consultant needs to be an architect of new systems and help the leader build the new systems.

The Stages of Team Development. The stages of team development — Formation, Familiarity, Power, Performance, and Synergy — provide a useful model for assessing a team.

The Formation Stage involves the practical and psychological "start-up" of the team. The challenge faced by a team in the Formation Stage is to create a team identity and to make the team important to the team members. A team in the Formation stage needs to establish its mission and operating procedures.

In the Familiarity Stage, members get to know one another. They begin to exchange opinions and disclose information. The challenge of the Familiarity Stage is for the team members to get to know each other, appreciate each other, and see each other as assets, not threats. A team in the Familiarity stage needs to encourage open communication among team members.

In the Power Stage, team members feel comfortable enough to disagree and express their feelings, often creating conflict. At the same time, team members often rebel against the team leader. As the team members get in touch with their own power, conflicts increase. The challenges faced by the team are to let everyone be heard, to express feelings productively rather than counterproductively, prevent factions and cliques, and foster creative communi-

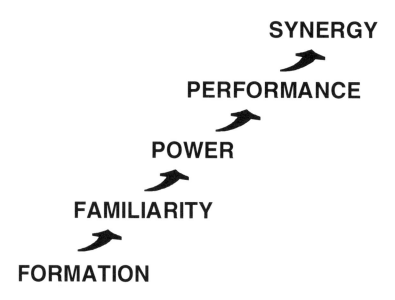

Figure 3.2 The Stages of Team Development

cation so that the "grapevine" isn't the primary communication line. A team in the Power stage needs to air differences and resolve conflicts.

In the Performance Stage, the team works together effectively and produces excellent performance. Members play off each other's strengths and successfully solve problems and make decisions. The challenge of the Performance Stage is to channel the skills, energy, and independent spirit of the team members into coordinated work. A team in the Performance stage needs to coordinate individual action and use the strengths of the members.

In the Synergy Stage, the team shows a high degree of unity and commitment to the team's mission. Members are energetic and enthusiastic. Members will often sacrifice for the sake of the team's performance. The challenge in the Synergy Stage is to maximize the power, connection, independence, and innovation of the team. A team in the Synergy stage needs to allow self-management by members and focus on long-term goals and resource needs.

The Building Blocks of Team Effectiveness. The building blocks of team effectiveness serve as a sequence of learnings and action steps for a team. Based on the chapters in *Continuous Improvement: Teams & Tools* by the authors of this book, the nine building blocks represent a blueprint for a team to operate in a customer-focused, process-oriented, team-based environment. The consultant can use the building blocks to determine what steps in training and implementation a team has already taken and what remains.

The first block (PDEI Continuous Improvement Cycle & Leadership

Requirement) focuses on today's new organizational paradigms, the concept of continuous improvement, and the organization's vision, mission, and principles. A team must understand today's new paradigms of quality, customer focus, and speed. A team must also understand how the continuous improvement cycle can be applied at the organizational, team, or individual level. A team should also have a deep appreciation of the vision, mission, and principles of the organization and how its work relates to those declarations.

The second block is the Team Charter. The team charter defines the specifics of a team's customer-supplier relationships. In its team charter, a

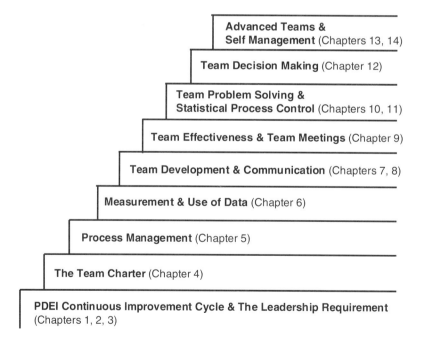

Figure 3.3 The Building Blocks of Team Effectiveness

team defines its unique mission and identifies the processes that the team operates to produce products and services.

The third block is Process Management. In the process approach, work is defined as a set of activities that transforms inputs into products and services to meet customer expectations. A team identifies and maps its processes, as well as plans and implements process improvement strategies.

The fourth block is Measurement. A team must determine how to track its performance against customer expectations, as well as the performance of its processes. Teams should track quantity, quality, cost, and time, defining measures in terms of ratios, ratings, or absolute numbers.

The fifth block is Team Development and Communication. Every team must negotiate the five stages of development: formation, familiarity, power, performance, and synergy (described above). Communication is the lubricant of continuous improvement. Team members must have the skills to tap the full potential of the talents and ideas of the team.

The sixth block is Team Effectiveness. A team must adopt certain disciplines for effective operation, particularly in the area of team meetings. Meeting disciplines include focusing agenda items on important issues, addressing issues in the time allotted, and documenting action items and decisions.

The seventh block is Team Problem Solving and Statistical Process Control. Methods of organized thinking in teams, as well as tools for analyzing and solving problems, are needed. Tools include cause-and-effect diagrams, force-field analysis, and Pareto analysis. A basic statistical foundation must be established so that a team can develop appropriate and useful control charts.

The eighth block is Team Decision Making. Making good decisions on a team is as much about "sound thinking" as it is about participation and ownership. A team should use tools of decision making to foster participation and analyze alternatives.

The ninth block is Advanced Teams and Self-Management. A team's evolution never stops. A team should define an ideal state of operation and aim toward it. Ultimately quality, has implications at the individual level — a team should help its members be the best they can be.

The McKinsey 7-S Framework. Peters and Waterman, in *In Search of Excellence,* described the McKinsey 7-S Framework as the basic diagnostic model by which they observed and discussed excellent companies. The seven S's are: Strategy, Structure, Systems, Style, Staff (people), Skills, and Shared Values. A variety of derivative models have appeared as many consultants have adopted the basic framework. *Strategy* refers to the organization's plan for success. *Structure* refers to the layers of management, spans of control, team configuration from top to bottom, and job design. *Systems* refer to the hard and soft systems that affect performance, including technical, financial, performance management, recognition and reward, compensation, communication and information, decision-making, and workforce planning and hiring. *Style* refers to the prevalent management style, cultural characteristics, and typical intra-group and inter-group dynamics, particularly personal communication styles and allocation of decision-making authority. **Staff** refers to the people of the organization, their capabilities, will, and experience. *Skills* refer to the "hard" and "soft" competencies that associates need to operate processes effectively. *Shared Values* refer to the organization's guiding principles, its basic culture, and the everyday cues that prompt cultural behavior (such as whether managers and nonmanagers have access to performance information, dress differently, and so forth). Although the 7-S framework may qualify as an "oldie-but-goodie," it is an excellent model for categorizing observations, questions, and recommendations about an organization.

The GE Model. GE's organizational change model, described in Noel M. Tichy and Stratford Sherman's *Control Your Destiny or Someone Else Will,* and in Tichy's *Fortune* article "Revolutionize Your Company," identifies three fundamental building blocks of all organizations: *the technical system —* organizing people, capital, information, and technology to produce goods or services; *the political system —* allocating power, rewards, and career opportunities; and, *the cultural system —* the set of shared norms, beliefs, and values of the organization. The GE model also identifies three basic elements of the organization: strategy, structure, and human resource management. *Strategy* refers to the direction and goals of the organization. *Structure* refers to the configuration of units, hierarchy, and so forth. *Human resource management* refers to all of the systems that affect human performance. The three building blocks and the three basic elements produce a nine-cell matrix that allows further analysis. For example, what implications does our strategy have on our technical systems, political systems, and cultural systems?

The Malcolm Baldrige National Quality Award criteria. The seven categories of the Malcolm Baldrige National Quality Award are: Leadership, Information and Analysis, Strategic Quality Planning, Human Resource Development and Management, Management of Process Quality, Quality and Operational Results, and Customer Focus and Satisfaction. The Baldrige award application items are an excellent means of assessing the quality performance of the client's organization.

Phrases For Making Recommendations

A consultant must have some phrases that are comfortable "openers" for making recommendations. Some ways of phrasing recommendations are:

- "What would you think about collecting and charting data on the number of incoming phone calls?"
- "Have you thought about having shorter, more frequent team meetings?"
- "I'd like to suggest that you include more quality data in your e-mail messages to the team."
- "Let me propose some options for how to proceed..."
- "If you think about this meeting as your regular means of reviewing data, sharing information, and action planning, you might want to set up a second regular meeting especially for problem-solving."

Coaching

Some specific aspects of coaching include: prompting for progress, pinpointing specific behaviors for the client to continue or change, and giving positive and developmental feedback.

Prompting For Progress

A simple but important coaching step is to encourage the client to keep going. Progress in change is usually slower than anyone expects. Until new behaviors become habits, consultants need to remind and encourage clients to keep trying and to make progress. The following are comfortable, effective prompting phrases:

- "The next step your team needs to work on is to finish its customer survey."
- "The next agenda should include sharing the fishbone diagram on late deliveries and identifying the team's views of the most likely causes."
- "It is important to make progress on developing a data collection system for how team members are spending their time."
- "Your team has made progress in identifying possible problems to address. The areas you need to work on next are selecting one problem and applying the seven-step problem-solving model to it."
- "You don't have a list of possible process variables to measure completed at this point."

Pinpointing

Our language contains vivid words, rich in descriptions of feelings and motives. For example, if we observe a manager doing most of the talking in a meeting and announcing decisions that he or she has already made, we might describe that manager's style as "autocratic," "controlling," "dominant," or "commanding." Although the connotations and nuances among these words might let us draw subtle verbal distinctions, this language is not very useful for helping that manager change. Such descriptions usually assume internal "states and traits" of the other person.

"States and traits" refer to our tendency to make assumptions about a person's style, temperament, personality, talent, predispositions, attitude, or feelings. Such references are not helpful because, as consultants, we can do little to influence them. In fact, adjectives in general, such as "autocratic" or "controlling," are not very helpful in describing what to do differently. Imagine being told, "Be less autocratic." You would have to make several guesses about the meaning of "autocratic," what you did to earn that description, and what you should do differently.

Pinpointing behavior is describing desired or undesired action that is observable, countable, and specific. "Observable" refers to actions that can be seen or heard. "Countable" means that the behavior should be described concretely enough that you could count the number of times the behavior occurs. "Specific" means that two persons would get the same count if they were both observing the same behaviors at the same time.

For example, a desired trait might be to "be more facilitative." The desired behavior, when pinpointed, might be to "ask more questions." "Asking more questions" is observable, countable, and two observers would be likely to get the same count. Coaching is much more likely to be successful when the desired behavior is described this specifically. As another example, a desired trait might be to "be more consultative and less commanding." The desired pinpointed behavior might be to "have team members give their opinions first and give yours last."

Feedback

A good coach must be able to give the client both positive and developmental feedback on his or her behavior. Positive feedback statements are comments like, "I thought you did a nice job of describing your customers' requirements in the team meeting." Developmental feedback statements are comments like, "I'd like to see you ask the team members in each meeting more about the data that they are collecting."

Positive feedback is usually not difficult to deliver. The key is to pinpoint the client's desirable behavior: "Something that you did that was particularly effective was to relate the team's questions back to the team charter." Developmental, or corrective, feedback can be more challenging. Developmental feedback can be quite short and simple:

- "I'd like to suggest that you share the agenda with the team 24 hours before the meeting."
- "I thought that the discussion got off-track. Next time you might want to get the team members to list pro's and con's and ask if they can agree on a decision."
- "I'd like to ask you to watch out about cutting people off in mid-sentence. That happened twice and those individuals were silent after that."

Feedback should be specific and immediate. Always pinpoint the behavior you are giving feedback on. Avoid generalizations, interpretations, and assumptions. Give the feedback as immediately as possible after you see the behavior.

In some situations, a fuller feedback statement may be needed. If you suspect that the client will not understand why a certain behavior is a problem or will be defensive, you may want to expand your feedback statement. A fuller feedback statement describes the undesirable behavior and its impact, asks for an alternative behavior, and describes the benefits of that new behavior. A fuller model for giving feedback would look like this:

Opener: "There's something I wanted to mention."

Empathy: "I can understand how you might feel (client's feeling)."

Pinpoint: "At the same time, I feel that you sometimes (undesired behavior)."

Result: "That sometimes leads to (undesired result)."

Pinpoint: "Can I ask you to (desired behavior)."

Benefit: "I think that would help (desired result)."

For example, if a client repeatedly responds to a consultant's suggestions by saying, "We do that already," the consultant may decide to give the client feedback about this habit:

Opener: "There's something I wanted to mention."

Empathy: "I can understand how you might feel that you do all this already."

Pinpoint: "At the same time, I feel that you sometimes say that before I even describe a particular topic."

Result: "That sometimes leads to dismissing the topic before we even talk about it."

Pinpoint: "Can I ask you to let me describe a topic first?"

Benefit: "I think that would help us find things that might add value to what you are already doing."

A phrase that helps in feedback discussions is "at the same time." Consultants often feel awkward saying the word "but": "I know that your team doesn't want to meet, *but* the team will not mature unless it gets together and communicates." The phrase "at the same time" is accurate and less awkward: "I know that your team doesn't want to meet, *at the same time* the team will not mature unless it gets together and communicates."

Phrases to avoid during feedback discussions are "always" and "never." The statements, "You *always* seem to start generating solutions before identifying the causes of a problem," or "You *never* review performance data in your team meetings," are bound to cause defensiveness. It is better to say, "I think you *sometimes* start generating solutions before identifying the causes of a problem," and "I notice that you *tend* not to review performance data in your team meetings."

Persuasion

Persuasion refers to describing a recommendation in terms of both its features and benefits to the client. We also include negotiating on the specifics of a recommendation in the category of persuasion.

Features And Benefits

Persuasion is convincing a client to accept a recommendation by describing its features and benefits. The premise behind describing features and benefits is that people usually don't buy something because: a) they don't understand what it is or how it works, or b) they don't see how it will meet their needs and goals. Features describe the former, and benefit statements describe the latter.

Features are the characteristics of what the consultant is advocating. Features answer the question, "What is it?" For example, if a consultant is attempting to convince a client to begin having team meetings, the features of team meetings are regularly scheduled meetings with agendas and action records, in which the team reviews action items and performance, shares information and recognition, does problem solving and decision making, and plans new action.

In the world of automobiles, if a feature is "four-wheel independent suspension," the benefit to the driver is "a smooth ride." Benefits describe why

Features	**Benefits**
• The characteristics of what I'm advocating	• Why it's good and how it's going to help me
• Answers the question: "What is it?"	• Answers the question: "So what?"
• Features of *Team meetings* -	• Benefits of *Team meetings* -
• Regularly scheduled meetings	• Improves communication
• With agendas, action records	• Keeps the team on track
• Team reviews action items and performance, shares info and recognition, does problem solving and decision making, and plans new action	• Avoids problems
	• Helps you meet your goals

Figure 3.4 Features and Benefits of Team Meetings

"To change your mind

and to follow him

who sets you right is

to be nonetheless

the free agent that

you were before."

Marcus Aurelius,

Roman emperor and

philosopher

the features are good and how they are going to help the buyer. Benefits answer the question, "So what?" In the above example of team meetings, the benefits to the client of team meetings are that team meetings improve communication, thus keeping the team on track, thus avoiding problems, and thus helping the team meet its goals.

When it is time to be persuasive, consultants must remember to emphasize benefit statements. Consultants often find the features of their recommendations intrinsically beneficial; in other words, the consultant is often convinced by the features themselves. For example, a consultant may find the features of quality function deployment (analysis of customer and technical requirements, ratings of importance, competitive comparisons, and so forth) obviously valuable and may describe them to the client in loving detail. Those same features may seem like a lot of detailed paperwork to the client. The consultant must connect the features of QFD to *benefits for the client.* In this case, QFD helps the team figure out how to translate the customer's desires into work specifications, where to get the most "improvement bang for its buck," and how to build in quality upfront to a service or product so there are fewer problems, and fewer headaches.

Phrases for persuasion can be quite straightforward. Consider these two examples:

- "What about trying electronic team meetings? In an electronic team meeting, the team members would add their input on action items, performance review, information-sharing, recognition, problems, and plans into a common notes file that each member could access. The benefits will be less meeting time, more involvement of distant members, and more flexibility of scheduling. What do you think?"

- "Would you try joint team meetings between sales and operations for a couple of months and see if they are helpful? Joint team meetings would involve members of both teams attending the same meetings to discuss common goals and problems. The benefits would be improved communication, less tension, and more problems solved early before they become big problems. Would you give that a try?"

Once the client has bought into the consultant's fundamental recommendation, it may be important to negotiate the specifics of implementing the recommendation. In other words, the consultant should persuade on the "what" of the recommendation and negotiate on the "how."

Negotiation

Negotiation is working out a win-win agreement that meets both sets of true interests. Roger Fisher and William Ury, in *Getting to Yes: Negotiating Agreement Without Giving In,* and Ury, in *Getting Past No: Negotiating Your Way From Confrontation To Cooperation,* have offered a basic model for negotiation based on identifying the needs behind stated positions. A **position** is my current statement of what I want. A **need**, or **interest**, is my true motive or desire. For example, a consultant might suggest that a team track four process variables on a regular basis. That is the consultant's stated position. The consultant's real interest is that the team track data to ensure that the team's processes are in control; "tracking four process variables" is a representation of that need. The client may state that the team only has time to track two variables. That is the client's position. The client's real interest may be that tracking data should not intervene with the team's ability to get its work done and operate the process. Rather than resort to "positional bargaining," in which the consultant and client both attempt to win their positions (four versus two variables) or compromise (at three variables), effective negotiation would focus on both sets of interests. What options might exist to meet the consultant's need to ensure that data are collected for process control, and the client's need for the team to have time to get its work done? A variety of options, such as: automatic data collection, tracking one variable at a time, data collection by a non-team member, additional training on data collection, and so forth. Any one of these options may appear once the consultant and client discuss their true interests.

The steps in win-win negotiation are:

1. Listen for the person's position and needs. For example, imagine that your client has consented to regular meetings and you are now discussing the appropriate frequency. You might begin by listening to the client's side: "How often do you think we should meet to maintain good consultant-client communication?"

2. State your position and needs. In our example, you might say, "I'd like us to meet once a week. What's important to me is that we have regular, frequent contact so that I can share with you what's happening, you can give me your perspective, and I can ask you for your help when I need it."

3. Identify options that meet both needs. In this example, options may include having coffee once a week, having frequent phone, voice mail, or e-mail contact, meeting before or after work, and so forth.

If the client seems reluctant to negotiate, ask questions such as:
* "What's driving your position?"
* "What's important to you?"
* "What if we met before work?"

To attempt win-win negotiation with a reluctant client, offer the best alternative that seems to meet the client's real needs, without jeopardizing your real need: "What I could do is chart your team's data myself, but I would like to train someone at the same time to meet my need to transfer the skills to the team."

Confronting

Confronting includes naming the resistance and disagreeing.

Naming The Resistance

Naming the resistance is calmly labeling the resistant behavior that you observe. As Peter Block observed in *Flawless Consulting,* in traditional organizations, many of us learned to pretend to avoid punishment — to act like we're happy when we're not, act like we support something when we don't, and act like we're getting what we need when we're not. Both the client and the consultant can fall into this trap. The client can start pretending that he or she is actively participating in the change, and the consultant can start pretending not to notice that the client is pretending! Naming the resistance is the consultant's way of saying out loud what's really going on. The premise behind confronting is that it is better to be straightforward (even if it's temporarily uncomfortable) than to pretend. Consider the following examples:

- If the client seems to be balking at starting an action plan, the consultant might say, "You seem reluctant to proceed with the project."
- If the client has postponed several meetings, the consultant might say, "You've canceled our last three meetings."
- If the client is showing signs of resistance, the consultant might say, "You don't seem like you're buying this."
- If the client seems dissatisfied or angry, the consultant might say, "You seem concerned about how the process is going."

When naming the resistance, use a gentle tone of voice, good eye contact, and silence after your statement. Whatever the client says in response to you naming the resistance is probably quite genuine and certainly important information for your consultant-client relationship.

Disagreeing

Disagreeing is differing with the client in a straightforward, open manner. When the client makes a statement in direct opposition to the principles or approach of the change effort, the consultant must make it clear that he or she has a different view.

Some phrases that can make disagreement more comfortable are:

- "I am going to disagree with you and let me tell you why..."
- "I think you could look at that another way."

- "I look at that differently. It seems to me that not every group is a true team."
- "Something that worries me about that is that the team is making decisions in the absence of data."
- "Let me try to sell you on another view on that."

Solving

To solve problems effectively, a consultant needs a general problem-solving model and a performance-analysis model. A general problem-solving model is described earlier in this chapter and in *Continuous Improvement: Teams & Tools* by the authors of this book.

An excellent performance-analysis model was provided by Mager and Pipe in *Analyzing Performance Problems, or You Really Oughta Wanna.* Mager and Pipe suggest the following series of steps in analyzing problems in human performance:

1. Pinpoint the performance deficiency. A performance deficiency is a discrepancy between the desired behaviors and the behaviors that are actually occurring. Describe behaviors in pinpointed fashion, avoiding references to internal traits such as "autocratic" or "intimidating." For example, a consultant defines a performance gap in which a client is not using open-ended questions, prompting, and rephrasing to draw out participation in meetings.

2. Decide if the performance deficiency is worth the effort of solving it. If the behavior is your client's, ask yourself, "Is this worth addressing with my client?" If the client has asked for advice about the behavior of others, ask, "How important is this performance?" In our example, not drawing out participation in meetings is worth addressing.

3. Decide if it's "skill" or "will." In other words, is the problem a skill deficiency or a motivational deficiency? Ask yourself, "If I gave this person $1,000,000 to change this behavior, would they do it?" If $1,000,000 (or any high-magnitude motivation) would not improve the performance, it is a "Can't Do" problem. If $1,000,000 would improve the performance, it is a "Won't Do" problem.

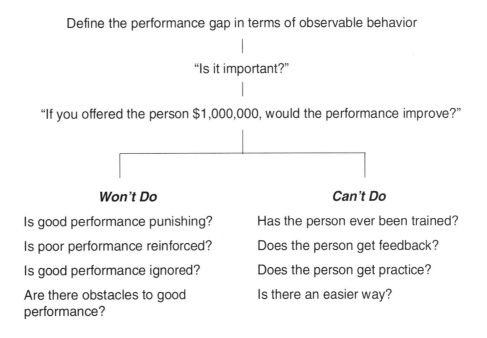

Define the performance gap in terms of observable behavior

"Is it important?"

"If you offered the person $1,000,000, would the performance improve?"

Won't Do	*Can't Do*
Is good performance punishing?	Has the person ever been trained?
Is poor performance reinforced?	Does the person get feedback?
Is good performance ignored?	Does the person get practice?
Are there obstacles to good performance?	Is there an easier way?

Figure 3.5 The Performance Analysis Model (adapted from the work of Mager and Pipe)

In our example, let's assume that the consultant decides that the failure to draw out participation is a "Won't Do" problem. If you have a "Won't Do" performance problem, Mager and Pipe suggest these questions to identify the possible causes and determine appropriate solutions.

4. Is the desired behavior punishing? Sometimes, doing a desired behavior has unpleasant results for a person. If asking for customer feedback has produced negative feedback in the past, a team may be hesitant to seek additional feedback. In our example, if drawing out team members' opinions has led to unpleasant arguments in the past, a team leader may be reluctant to open up topics for discussion. The solution is to arrange for positive reinforcement of the desired behavior.

5. Is the undesired behavior reinforcing? If a person encounters pleasant consequences for the undesired behavior, he or she may continue that behavior. For instance, an individual who has solved problems without data or analysis may continue this approach and may not be motivated to use problem-solving techniques. In our example, if announcing decisions with little discussion from the team has felt good, the client may be motivated to continue that approach.

6. Is the desired behavior ignored? People may become less motivated if doing the desired behavior does not receive any acknowledgment or credit. For instance, a team that embraces quality techniques but doesn't see results or obtain recognition may stop using the techniques. In our example, the client may not draw out participation because no one has said anything one way or the other when he has done so in the past. In other words, if drawing out participation has not mattered, the client may be likely to stop.

7. Are there obstacles to, or no prompts for, the desired behavior? People may become less motivated if it is difficult to do the desired behavior or if expectations are unclear. For instance, if the implementation of team meetings required additional paperwork, team members may gradually have fewer meetings, or shortcut the paperwork. In our example, if the team's meetings are scheduled for only 30 minutes, the team leader may be reluctant to open up discussion.

Now let's assume that the consultant decides that the failure to draw out participation is a "Can't Do" problem. If you have a "Can't Do" performance deficiency, ask these questions to identify the possible causes and determine appropriate solutions.

8. Has the person ever been trained? If a person has a skill deficiency and has never been competent, the person probably requires training. For instance, a consultant may observe that a team leader does not facilitate a brainstorming session skillfully. The consultant may realize that the team leader has never had problem-solving training and has tried to learn it by trial-and-error. In our example, it may be that the client missed the training on facilitating participation. The solution would be training or individual coaching.

9. Does the person get feedback? A person may become less skillful in the absence of positive or corrective comments about his or her performance. Without feedback, a person's behavior may "drift" from the original expectations or standards. For instance, a consultant may observe that a team leader's presentation on total quality has left out much of the original content. The presentation has diminished in the absence of feedback. The solution would be to increase the frequency and specificity of the feedback to the team leader. In our example, the client may have never received feedback on his meeting-leadership skills and may be unaware of any problem whatsoever.

10. Does the person get to practice? A person can become less skillful without the chance to practice. For instance, a team leader who once knew how to determine which type of control chart is appropriate for a given type of data may go for a year without selecting a new chart. When a new chart is needed, the team leader cannot correctly determine the appropriate type of chart. His skillfulness has decreased through lack of practice. The solution is to practice or review infrequently used skills. In our example, if meetings are infrequent, the client may simply not get enough opportunity to practice drawing out participation.

11. Is there an easier way? Sometimes a person can't do a task well as it is currently designed. A change in the design of the task, or the introduction of a new tool, may have a major impact on performance. For example, a job that requires both paper filing and computer filing could perhaps be made more doable if the need for paper files were eliminated.

Questions to be considered in looking for an easier way include: Can the methods and procedures be improved? Can the tools and equipment be upgraded or made easier to use? Can the work be made simpler, more streamlined, or more convenient? Can the scheduling of work be improved? Can the materials in the task be changed or handled differently?

12. Finally, the consultant must ask: Does the person have the potential to do these particular tasks? If the job cannot be made easier, and if, after training, practice, and feedback, a person still cannot do the desired behavior, the potential may not be there.

Mager and Pipe's model reminds the consultant not to be too smart for one's own good. It is an occupational hazard for a consultant to invent ten smart, complex reasons why a team or individual isn't functioning well. Instead, "dumbly" identify the simple, main cause of the performance gap and try to fix it. Don't overanalyze the problem. Many a facilitator has attributed a team's problem to the personality deficits of various members only to have it pointed out that the team never received any training or feedback. Look for "simple" answers to performance gaps first, such as training, one-to-one follow-up, involvement of the leader, open communication, goals and measures, feedback, recognition, or resources. Make sure that those solutions have been tried before you look for fancy, complicated answers. (Save your theory that they need primal-scream therapy for last.)

Summary

In this chapter we have described the basic skill sets of consulting: listening, planning, contracting, and advising. The advising skill set was further divided into recommending, coaching, persuading, confronting, and solving. In the next chapter, we will look at the Evaluation step in the consulting cycle in detail.

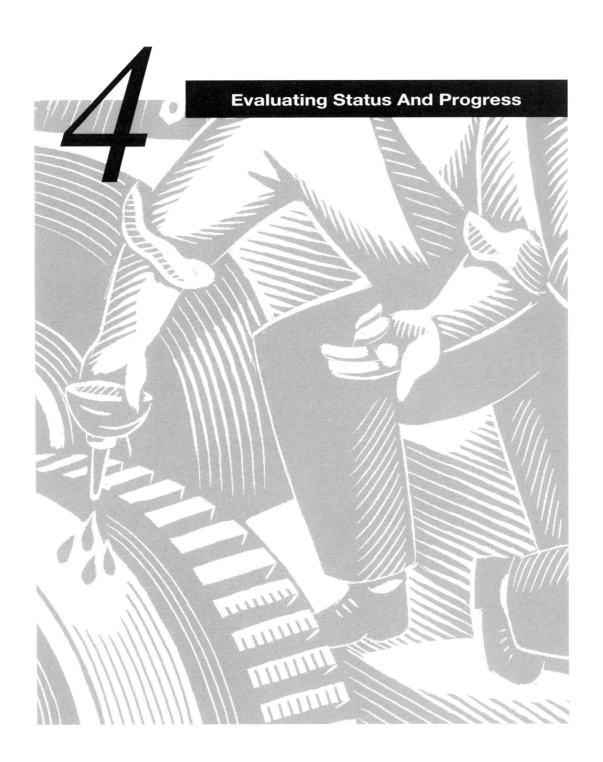

4

4

What To Evaluate

How To Evaluate

Evaluating Status And Progress

The logical first step in the consulting cycle is Evaluation. Evaluation means assessing the effectiveness of the organization and its current environment. Evaluation is answering the question: "What's going on?"

In this chapter, we will describe the basics of effective evaluation in a consulting situation and offer a number of evaluation tools. We will focus both on what the consultant should evaluate and how to do so.

What To Evaluate

The consultant should evaluate three key elements during an assignment: 1) the performance of the organization, 2) the progress of the change effort, and 3) the effectiveness of the consulting interventions.

The Performance Of The Organization

A fundamental, but sometimes overlooked, type of evaluation is evaluating the organization's results. How is the organization performing? Consultants often fail to evaluate the organization's business performance for three reasons. First, they believe that the organization's performance is not relevant to the desired intervention. For example, a consultant who is delivering a teambuilding service may feel that the team's interactions, not the business results of the organization, are relevant. Second, a consultant's expertise may not be in "hard numbers" (finance or business analysis), so he or she may not be sure how to evaluate organizational performance. Third, a consultant may simply not be aware of the organization's business results and may be timid about asking.

Evaluating organizational performance is important because "business results" are the context in which change happens. To stay grounded in reality, be relevant to leaders and managers, make connections between "soft" changes and the business, and ultimately help create permanent results, the consultant must keep one eye on the organization's business performance.

A consultant's contract may include helping the organization develop performance measures. To develop performance measures, you must identify: a) categories of measures, b) units of measures, and c) levels of measurement. Developing performance measures also includes defining how a particular unit of measure is calculated, as well as the source of the raw data and the method of data collection.

Categories Of Measures

Categories of measures are "what to measure." According to Masaaki Imai in *Kaizen: The Key to Japan's Competitive Success,* appropriate categories of performance measures are:

- quality
- cost
- scheduling (that is, the quantity and timing of delivery)

The American Productivity & Quality Center suggests measuring quality, productivity, timeliness, and cost. In *Continuous Improvement: Teams & Tools,* the authors suggest:

- quantity
- quality
- timeliness
- use of resources
- leadership

These basic categories of measures can and should be broken down into specific customer requirements. For example, David Garvin, in his *Harvard Business Review* article, "Competing on the Eight Dimensions of Quality," suggests the following customer requirements in the *quality* category:

- *Performance* — The product's primary operating characteristics
- *Features* — The "bells and whistles" that supplement the basic functioning
- *Reliability* — The probability of a product malfunctioning
- *Conformance* — The degree to which a product's design meets standards
- *Durability* — The product life in terms of economic and technical dimensions
- *Serviceability* — The speed, courtesy, competence, and ease of repair
- *Aesthetics* — How a product looks, feels, sounds, tastes, or smells
- *Perceived quality* — Inferences about quality reputation from images, advertising, or brand

A tree diagram (see Figure 4.1) can be helpful in breaking down the categories of measures into more and more specific measures of customer or company requirements. To create a tree diagram, start with a broadly-stated

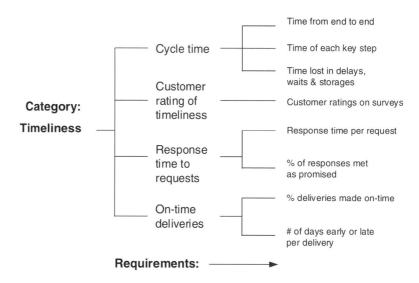

Figure 4.1 Tree Diagram Defining Requirements and Measures

requirement, then draw branches to delineate more specific requirements in finer and finer detail. In the figure, the requirement of timeliness is divided into process cycle time, customer ratings of timeliness, response time, and on-time deliveries. Each of these branches is then further subdivided. The tree diagram is a particularly powerful tool if the consultant and client construct it together.

Units Of Measurement

Units of measurement are "how" to measure. The units of measurement are ratios, ratings, and absolute numbers.

Ratios. Ratios indicate percent or rate. Examples of ratios are: percent on-time performance, percent of desired applicants hired, percent of customers

Customer Feedback Form

Priority		Usually does not meet expectations	Sometimes meets expectations	Usually meets expectations	Sometimes exceeds expectations	Usually exceeds expectations
_____	Our accessibility to you	_____	_____	_____	_____	_____
_____	Responsiveness to your requests	_____	_____	_____	_____	_____
_____	Timeliness of service	_____	_____	_____	_____	_____
_____	Reliability of products and services	_____	_____	_____	_____	_____
_____	Up-to-date products and services	_____	_____	_____	_____	_____
_____	Usefulness of our documentation	_____	_____	_____	_____	_____
_____	Usefulness of our technical support	_____	_____	_____	_____	_____
_____	Our complaint process	_____	_____	_____	_____	_____
_____	Our ability to solve your problems	_____	_____	_____	_____	_____
_____	Attitude of our personnel	_____	_____	_____	_____	_____
_____	Competence of our personnel	_____	_____	_____	_____	_____
_____	The clarity of our communication	_____	_____	_____	_____	_____
_____	Our integrity in dealing with you	_____	_____	_____	_____	_____
_____	Our understanding of your needs	_____	_____	_____	_____	_____
_____	Our value and price	_____	_____	_____	_____	_____

Figure 4.2 A Customer Feedback Form

returning for repeat orders, percent of team action items completed on-time, percent turnover, percent rework, percent of employee time in training, percent of team goals met, percent of work which is scheduled in advance, percent of jobs interrupted, percent of jobs whose scope is changed after starting, percent attendance, percent above or below budget, and percent overtime.

Ratings. Ratings indicate satisfaction or perception. Customer ratings are usually along a numerical scale. In Figure 4.2, dimensions of quality are listed in a customer feedback form. The customer is asked to rate the team on each dimension and to rank the dimensions in terms of their importance. The customer can complete the survey regularly (for example, quarterly) to give the team numerical indicators of its performance in meeting customer requirements.

Absolute numbers. Absolute numbers indicate occurrences over time. Examples are: numbers of customer complaints, repeat customers, new customers, training courses completed, technical conferences attended, equipment failures, new methods developed, downtime due to equipment failures, and time needed to turn a job around. Absolute numbers also include the cost of savings and value added in dollar terms.

Levels Of Measures

Levels of measures are the "why" of measurement. Levels of measurement include mission measures, process output measures, and process variable measures.

Mission Measures. Mission measures are the business results that the team directly impacts. Mission measures are the indicators of the organization's fundamental accomplishments as a business. If the organization has stated its mission, then mission measures are the quantitative indicators of its success against it. Mission measures include indicators of cost, quality, speed, customer satisfaction, employee satisfaction, revenue, and profitability.

Process output measures. Process output measures are measures of the outputs of an organization, or a team's work processes. Process output measures are used to track the products or services of an operation. Process output measures drive mission measures. Examples of process output are the number of reports generated, number of requests processed, number of projects finished, and number of projects meeting deadlines. Figure 4.3 shows examples of process output measures organized by category and unit of measure.

Process Output Measures by Category

Units / Categories	Ratios	Ratings	Absolute Numbers
Quantity	Output/Input Weighted Output/Input	Team's Rating of Progress on Goals	# Reports # Publications # Proposals # Patents, etc. vs. Team's Goal
Quality	# Defects/Output Rework/Output Retention Rate	Customer Satisfaction Ratings	# Complaints & Compliments # Suggestions # Improvements
Timeliness	On Schedule/ Total Output Cycle Time Turn-around Time	Customer Satisfaction Ratings	# Ideas for Speed # Ideas Acted on
Use of Resources	Net Present Value/ Net Present Cost Resources Used/Available Costs vs. Budget	Team's Rankings of Opportunities for Efficiencies	# Ideas for Efficiencies # Ideas Acted on
Leadership	Mgt $/Non-mgt $ # Mgrs/# Non-mgrs	Employee Satisfaction Ratings Upward Appraisals	# Trained # Recognitions # System Improvements

Figure 4.3 Examples of process output measures by measurement category.

Process output measures include nontraditional measures such as the cost of quality. The cost of quality is the price an organization pays for the nonconformance of its goods and services. It is the cost of doing things wrong. The price of nonconformance is the total money wasted on nonconforming activities, and outcomes, such as rework, scrap, expediting, unplanned service, repeat service, reruns, downtime, warranty work, "just-to-be-safe" inventory, and appeasements for customer complaints.

Process variable measures. Process variable measures are measures that indicate the performance of a process itself, before outputs are produced. Process variable measures are used to maintain and improve quality by tracking the process. Examples of process variables might be the number of calls answered within 20 seconds, whether a needs assessment was done prior to training, or the analysis of time taken to produce a first draft of proposal.

The Progress Of The Change Effort

Measures of the actions of the participants are basically the percent of teams or individuals that have achieved a particular accomplishment. For example, a consultant might measure the percent of teams or individuals showing positive results or passing a certain milestone, such as: identifying customer requirements, defining key processes, defining team measures, establishing goals, or implementing action plans.

If the consultant is assisting in the implementation of a team system, possible measures of progress include the number of employees involved in natural work teams and process improvement teams, as well as the percent of team meetings that are held as scheduled. If a suggestion system is being implemented, some measures of progress could be the number of suggestions offered per time-period, the percent of suggestions actually implemented, and the dollar value of implemented suggestions (in total and per suggestion).

The Effectiveness Of Consulting Interventions

Possible measures of the consulting process are: percent of client contracts completed, percent of consulting contacts made as scheduled, number or percent of team meetings attended as scheduled, number of times feedback is provided to the leaders, percent of status reports completed on time, percent of employees trained, and client satisfaction.

Figure 4.4 shows a sample feedback form that the consultant can use to obtain client feedback and track client satisfaction over time.

How To Evaluate

The consultant's methods of evaluation include: 1) reviewing performance data (described above), 2) conducting customer and organizational surveys, 3) interviewing individuals or focus groups, and 4) making firsthand observations.

Customer Surveys

The tools of customer satisfaction research include: telephone surveys, mail surveys, face-to-face interviews, 800 numbers, customer comment cards, "mystery shoppers," videotaping customer interactions, focus groups, benchmark studies, customer "field trips" in which employees visit customers, critical-incidents analysis, industry-wide surveys (such as J. D. Powers), direct

Client Feedback Form for Consultants

Please complete this form on your consultant. Use the following scale:

Client: _____ Consultant: _____

1	2	3	4	5
Rarely		Usually Does		Almost Always

Coaching

_____ 1. Gives me timely, frank, and candid feedback.

_____ 2. Coaches me to model appropriate practices.

_____ 3. Provides a "road map" in the quality process.

_____ 4. Meets with me before and after each team meeting.

_____ 5. Offers constructive feedback, both positive and developmental.

_____ 6. Negotiates win/win situations.

_____ 7. Conducts coaching sessions that reflect planning and preparation.

Communication

_____ 8. Communicates a positive vision of the future of the organization.

_____ 9. Practices active listening with me.

_____ 10. Speaks and writes clearly, concisely and accurately.

_____ 11. Ensures that I am aware of the priorities in the implementation.

Effectiveness

_____ 12. Brings new ideas to my team.

_____ 13. Helps me prepare new ideas for implementation.

_____ 14. Models quality principles and practices.

_____ 15. I look to my consultant for advice.

_____ 16. Has developed some knowledge of my business.

_____ 17. Has the necessary skills to help my team and me.

Availability

_____ 18. Responds to customer requests within two working days.

_____ 19. Is available when needed.

_____ 20. Meets deadlines we have agreed upon.

Figure 4.4 Client Feedback Form

observation of service events, subsequent customer actions, customer comment cards, and actual performance against service standards. As Ron Zemke and Dick Schaaf note in *The Service Edge: 101 Companies That Profit from Customer Care,* "Among the Service 101, we found that the measurement of service performance is a systematic effort that depends on no single measure to tell all. These organizations seem to wear both belts and suspenders, just in case. They value 'non-repetitive, redundant' measures of frontline performance, customer satisfaction, and service quality — they measure the same thing in a lot of different ways."

Planning A Customer Survey

The issues in planning a customer survey include determining to whom, and how many, to survey, the frequency of the survey, and the types of questions to ask.

Determining whom to survey. Recipients of a customer survey can be current customers, new customers, prospective customers, former customers, and customers of competitors. Members of the distribution chain can also be surveyed.

The number of customers surveyed. A census survey is one in which all customers are surveyed. Often surveys are given to a random sample of customers. The typical size of a sample is between 100, which is minimum, and 1,000. A stratified sample is one which targets a certain number within a specific segment of the customer population. A judgment sample is one based on the researcher's judgment of the industry or market.

The frequency of surveying. The frequency of surveying varies by industry, company, and the cycle time for data collection and analysis. Typically, surveys are done quarterly, or every six months. One commonality of effective customer surveys is that surveying is done on a regular basis, not as a one-shot occurrence.

Types of questions. Questions can be open-ended, close-ended, or multiple-choice. They can include ranking and rating scales and checklists. Questions can ask for overall perceptions, attribute ratings, paired comparisons, quality ratings, satisfaction ratings, and value ratings. Attribute ratings measure specific attributes of service (see Figure 4.2). Paired comparison questions ask, "Which of these two factors is more important to you...?" A customer can be asked to rate quality, satisfaction, and value. For example, in a restaurant, a quality rating question would ask, "How would you rate the quality of the meal served at this restaurant?" A satisfaction rating question would ask, "How satisfied were you with the meal served at this restaurant?" A value rating question would ask, "Do you feel you received a good meal for the price you paid?"

Organizational Surveys

Organizational surveys can be used to reach a large number of associates in a short period of time. They can identify areas for further study or confirm findings obtained through other means. Organizational surveys are beneficial because:

- They are relatively inexpensive to administer.
- Survey items can be easily constructed.

- Survey results can be reported quantitatively and objectively.
- Associates can give information freely and confidentially.

The most important purposes of organizational surveys are to: a) obtain baseline data, b) compare the present to the desired vision, c) surface areas for improvement, and d) identify possible solutions and interventions.

Categories Of Items

We suggest organizational survey items in the following categories:

- Culture/climate
- Leadership practices
- Decision-making and empowerment
- Problem-solving
- Team effectiveness and meetings
- Team development and communication
- Measurement, goals, and feedback
- Processes and procedures
- Customers

Sample Items

The following are sample survey items in the recommended categories.

Culture/Climate: "I feel free to tell my manager what I think."

Leadership Practices: "My manager lets me know what is expected of me."

Decision-Making and Empowerment: "My manager lets me do my job without interfering."

Problem-Solving: "Problems that are identified on our team are quickly solved."

Team Effectiveness and Meetings: "My manager lets me know when I've done a good job."

Team Development and Communication. "My manager is willing to listen to my concerns."

Measurement, Goals, and Feedback. "My work group emphasizes meeting its objectives successfully."

Processes and Procedures. "Rules and procedures do not interfere with how well I am able to do my job."

Customers. "My work group is involved in activities to improve service to our group's customers."

Guidelines For Organizational Surveys

Surveys should not be used alone. They should serve as stimuli for further fact-finding and analysis. Survey results should be processed with participants in facilitated feedback sessions, and action plans should be developed to respond to issues raised. We recommend that surveys be about 30 questions in length. Questions should be worded clearly and not be "tricky." "Agree" should signify an affirmation of the item statement. We suggest a five-point Likert scale: Strongly Agree—Agree—Sometimes Agree/Disagree—Disagree—Strongly Disagree. Items should refer to the respondent's frame of reference by using the pronouns "I," "me," "we," "us," or "our." Items should contain single statements, avoiding the word "and." For example, "We do our work quickly and without errors" is a poor item because it is a double statement. Items should avoid absolutes, such as "always" or "never."

Interviews

One of the most common evaluation methods for consultants is interviewing. Interviews are used to:

- Gather information at the beginning of the change effort.
- Supplement and validate the information from surveys.
- Identify causes of organizational problems and possible solutions.
- Involve the clients and consultants jointly in evaluating the current state of the organization.

Interviewing also serves to give the consultant a personal feel for the culture and the associates' feelings and reactions. Interviewing often serves as an "icebreaker" as it is usually the first time the consultant is seen by the participants in the consulting role.

Planning To Interview

The American Society for Training and Development suggests that you conduct four to six interviews when studying a homogeneous group. Most of the information tends to be gathered in the first few interviews. Interviews should be conducted in private, comfortable surroundings, such as a conference room or the client's office. Have a plan for conducting the interview; know what questions you want to ask in advance.

Conducting The Interview

Let the participants know the purpose of the interviews, how the information will be used, and the level of anonymity of their answers. Describe the procedures for note-taking, or taping, and how the notes or tapes will be used.

Make sure the participant is comfortable with it. Begin with general questions and work up to more specific ones. Maintain your objectivity. If you are taking notes, get all the facts accurately. Do not allow your biases to prevent accurate note-taking. Agree to any requests for "off-the-record" comments. Use good listening and keep the interview on track; stick to your time schedule. Most interviews are open-ended, however you can add specificity to any open-ended interview by asking the person to answer a specific question, such as "Would you say the level of stress on your team is high, medium, or low?" End the interview by thanking the participant and reviewing how the information will be used.

Focus Groups

Use focus groups when group interactions are important for job performance and when you want to learn how work gets done. Use individual interviews when you want to learn more specific, personal opinions and impressions about the culture.

Interview Or Focus Group Questions

The following are effective questions for interviewing one-to-one or in focus groups.

Overview

1. What is your job? That is, what are your major responsibilities?
2. What, in your view, are the major strengths, resources, and capabilities of your team?
3. What, in your view, are the major areas for improvement for your team? What are the vulnerabilities of your team, or constraints, that it is facing?

Culture

1. What is it like to work here?

2. What activities take up most of your time?

3. Draw a "map" of the other work units you interact with to get your work done. How effective are these interactions? How good is the communication?

4. If I were just starting out here and I asked you, "What do I have to do to be successful around here," what would you tell me?

5. What does your boss do that helps you do your job?

6. How could he or she be more effective in supporting your job?

7. On a scale from 1 (no teamwork) to 10 (everyone works together whenever necessary), where would you place your team?

8. On a scale from 1 (no teamwork) to 10 (everyone works together whenever necessary), where would you place the senior team of this organization?

Organizational History

1. Has there been any reorganization or other major organizational changes during the last few years that have affected you and your work? Tell me about it.

2. Over the last couple of years, what efforts have been made to improve quality, cost, speed, customer satisfaction, or employee satisfaction? What impact have these activities had? If they have failed or stalled, why?

Team Charter

1. How do you define the mission of your team? In other words, what are your team's business activities?

2. Who are your major customers? What do you supply them?

3. In your team, how would you define success? What are the critical success factors that determine success?

4. How well does your team do each of these critical success factors? What measures do you use to tell you that?

5. What are your major objectives for this year?

6. What are the most critical problems or issues facing your team in the next 12 months? Beyond the next 12 months?

7. When a problem arises, how does your team typically handle it? What is your team's approach to problem-solving?

Critical Processes

1. If your team (or organization) was to focus on a small number of specific work processes to improve in the next year, which work processes would you most like to see selected? For each process identified, ask:

   Why is that an important process?

   Can you describe an example of what goes wrong?

   Why isn't the process working as well as it should?

Conclusion

1. If you could change one thing around here, what would it be?

2. What would you like this change initiative to accomplish?

3. What could prevent that from happening?

4. What can I do as the internal consultant to make it successful?

5. Is there anything else you'd like to share that you think is important?

6. Do you have any questions for me?

Interview Questions For Executives

The following are effective questions for interviewing senior managers.

Overview

1. What is your job? What part of the organization are you in charge of?

2. What, in your view, are the major strengths, resources, and capabilities of your organization?

3. What, in your view, are the major areas for improvement for your team? What are the vulnerabilities of your team, or constraints, that it is facing?

4. What are the primary factors on which your customers judge your performance (for example, responsiveness, ability to solve problems, competence of personnel)?

Culture

1. What is it like to work here?

2. What activities take up most of your time?

3. If you could change one thing around here, what would it be?

4. Help us draw a "map" of the other work units you interact with to get your work done. How effective are these interactions? How good is the communication?

5. On a scale from 1 (we get in each other's way) to 10 (we all work together whenever necessary), where would you place the Senior Team?

6. Over the last couple of years, what efforts have been made to improve quality, cost, speed, customer satisfaction, or employee satisfaction? What impact have these activities had? If they have failed or stalled, why?

7. What is your view of the need for a change process?

8. In your view, what specific skills will be required in this organization in order to realize maximum benefit from this change initiative?

Business Issues

1. What are the desirable business results for your organization and for yourself as a member of the senior team?

2. Are these results systematically tracked and managed by you? How?

3. Have your business plan objectives changed significantly over the last few years?

4. In the near future, what major challenges, or issues, does your area face?

5. What other factors in the organization significantly impact the quality of products and services that you provide?

Critical Processes

1. If your work unit, or business line, were to focus on a small number of specific work processes to improve in the next year, which work processes would you most like to see selected? For each process identified, ask: Why is that an important process? Can you describe an example of what goes wrong? Why isn't the process working as well as it should?

Conclusion

1. What would you like this change initiative to accomplish in your area?

2. What could prevent that from happening?

3. What can I do as the consultant to make it successful?

4. Is there anything else you'd like to share that you think is important?

5. Do you have any questions for me?

Observation

Observation is directly watching the work behavior and interactions of people in the organization. Observation can be very powerful. In process analysis, there is no substitute for "stapling yourself to an invoice" and observing firsthand what happens to one unit of throughput. Some tips for effective observation are:

- Explain the purpose of the observations to the associates.

- Describe what you see with narrative statements or checklists.

- Quantify what you see as much as possible.

- Check the validity of what you see by comparing it to reports and discussing it with staff.

- Be thorough. Make your observations in one session a process, unless you are purposely returning to check observer reliability or sample.

- Be unobtrusive; do not intervene.

- Use a conceptual model to structure your observations. For example, use a process approach to observe work in action, or a team meeting model to observe a meeting.

- Look for "significant events," such as how the day starts, how a customer is communicated with, how a problem is handled, how a success is handled, how a meeting is run, how data is collected, or how managers and nonmanagers interact.

- Write down your observations fully as soon as possible after your observation session. Your observations will evaporate quickly.

- When you see something you don't understand, write down your question. Don't assume that there is a good reason for everything you see. You may be observing a problem situation that exists simply because "we've always done it that way."

A consultant can use observation to look for evidence of a specific phenomenon. Let's say that a consultant is evaluating an organization that has expressed interest in a quality improvement initiative. If quality is currently a focus of the organization, the consultant should be able to see indications of it. The consultant can evaluate the current emphasis on quality by making some common-sense observations:

- Are goals for quality posted or discussed?
- Are quality measures defined? Can you see evidence of a quality monitoring system? Are quality charts posted?
- Do senior managers hold reviews on quality? If you attend a meeting, is quality discussed?
- Do performance appraisal forms include quality? Do you see quality awards prominently displayed? Can you see evidence of other systems that seem to support quality performance?
- What are people, especially senior managers, actually doing with regard to quality? Do people talk about quality?

The answers to these questions must be confirmed through interviews. Nonetheless, sharp-eyed observation and awareness of what you are seeing, and *not* seeing, is a useful element of evaluation.

Summary

In this chapter we have described three key elements that a consultant should evaluate: 1) organizational performance, 2) progress of the change effort, and 3) the effectiveness of consulting interventions. We have also described four methods of evaluation: 1) reviewing performance data, 2) conducting organizational and customer surveys, 3) conducting interviews and focus groups, and 4) making observations. In the following chapter, we will examine Planning, the next step in the consulting cycle, in greater detail.

Addendum A: How Investors Evaluate

Investors consider at least six aspects of a company in judging its suitability as an investment: 1) company performance, 2) profitability, 3) financial strength, 4) management, 5) shareholder value, and 6) dividend payout ratio.

Company Performance

Is the company growing? To measure performance, investors look at top-line revenue. What has been the rate of growth in revenue? Investors like to see about five percent above the rate of inflation. Is the growth rate accelerating or decelerating? How does it compare to the competition? What has happened to revenue during economic slowdowns? What has happened in periods of prosperity? If the company isn't growing, why not? What is the effect of slowed, or no growth, on profitability? What is the company's plan of action?

Profitability

Is the company making money? To measure profitability, investors look at the company's income statement. What is the percentage of pretax profit on sales? Pretax profit is revenue on sales minus operating and interest expenses. Pretax profit allows more accurate comparisons since taxes vary. Investors like to see about a 10% profit margin. What is the company's profitability doing for the shareholder? What is the growth in earnings per share? Earnings per share is the total net income divided by the number of shares. Investors would like to see the earnings per share grow at the same rate as revenue.

Financial Strength

What does the company own and owe? To measure financial strength, investors look at the balance sheet. What are the assets of the company? How old are they? What are they really worth today? Investors usually like to see low debt and plenty of cash. If debt is taken on to fuel growth, can the company generate the cash flow to pay the interest? Is there regular turnover of inventory and accounts receivable? Is there any possible liability, such as from pending lawsuits?

Management

Is the company well run? To judge the management of the company, investors look at operating profit, that is, revenue on sales minus operating expenses. Are the senior managers doing every year what they say they want to do in the annual reports? Are they buying and holding stock? Is the senior team balanced, or is it an autocracy? Are the senior managers "innovators," "caretakers," or "undertakers"?

Shareholder Value

Can the company maximize shareholder wealth? A measure of shareholder value is the price/earnings ratio. Basically, investors look for low P/E ratios. If the P/E ratio is lower than the market, there may be opportunity — if there is earnings momentum and the price is still down. The higher the P/E ratio, the greater the confidence, but the less prospect of dramatic gain. Return on equity, another measure of shareholder value, is the percent return on the investors' capital. What is the return compared to putting the money in the bank? How does it compare to the market? Investors consider both market value and book value. Market value is the potential selling price of the assets. Book value is the listed value of the assets minus the liabilities on the balance sheet. Takeovers occur when someone thinks that the market value is substantially higher than the book value.

Dividend Payout Ratio

Dividends or increased equity? How much is paid out in dividends and how much is reinvested back in the business? The more growth, the less dividend, because the company wants to reinvest everything to fuel the growth. Some investors look for a safe investment that produces steady dividends. Other investors want a growth company that will significantly increase their equity.

Addendum B: Readings in Measurement

The following are useful readings on performance measurement.

Books

Boyett, Joseph H., and Henry P. Conn. *Maximum Performance Management.* Macomb, Illinois: Glenbridge Publishing, 1988.

Fitz-enz, Jac. *How to Measure Human Resources Management.* New York: McGraw-Hill, 1984.

Greif, Michel. *The Visual Factory.* Cambridge, Massachusetts: Productivity Press, Inc., 1991.

Lynch, Richard L, and Kelvin F. Cross. *Measure Up! Yardsticks for Continuous Improvement.* Cambridge, Massachusetts: Blackwell Publishers, 1991.

Lynch, Robert F., and Thomas J. Werner. *Continuous Improvement: Teams & Tools.* Milwaukee, Wisconsin: ASQC Quality Press, 1992.

Maskell, Brian H. *Performance Measurement for World Class Manufacturing.* Cambridge, Massachusetts: Productivity Press, Inc., 1991.

Sloma, Richard S. *How to Measure Managerial Performance.* New York: Macmillan Publishing Co., 1979.

Tally, Dorsey J. *Total Quality Management, Performance and Cost Measures: The Strategy for Economic Survival.* Milwaukee, Wisconsin: ASQC Quality Press, 1991.

Articles

American Productivity & Quality Center. "The Master Measurement Model of Employee Performance." *The SITE Foundation,* 32 pages.

Boyett, Joseph, and Henry Conn. "Developing White-Collar Performance Measures." *National Productivity Review,* Summer 1988, p. 109.

Cross, Kelvin F., and Richard L. Lynch. "Managing the Corporate Warriors." *Quality Progress,* April, 1990, pp. 54-59.

Garvin, David. "Competing on the Eight Dimensions of Quality." *Harvard Business Review,* 1987.

Kaplan, Robert S., and David P. Norton. "The Balanced Scorecard: Measures That Drive Performance." *Harvard Business Review,* January-February, 1992, pp. 71-79.

Kaplan, Robert S., and David P. Norton. "Putting the Balanced Scorecard to Work." *Harvard Business Review,* September-October, 1993, pp. 134-147.

Meyer, Christopher. "How the Right Measures Help Teams Excel." Harvard Business Review, May-June 1994, pp. 95-103.

Provost, Lloyd, and Susan Leddick. "How to Take Multiple Measures to Get a Complete Picture of Organizational Performance." *National Productivity Review,* Autumn, 1993, pp. 477-490.

Sullivan, Joanne M., and Robert F. Lynch. "Winning Teams Know Their Score." *Journal for Quality and Participation,* September, 1992, pp. 20-23.

Suminski, Leonard T., Jr. "Measuring the Cost of Quality." *Quality Digest,* March 1994, pp 26-32.

5

5

Planning For Change

The second step in the consulting cycle is planning. Logically, planning follows the Evaluation step. The consultant must determine what the client needs to do and how the client can help.

The purpose of this chapter is to describe models and tools for connecting the change effort to business planning, preparing for and managing a change effort, and assessing the levels of support among the stakeholders.

Why Change Efforts Succeed Or Fail

In many organizations people are cynical about change efforts because, in the past, the efforts have not lasted or produced results. Let's look at why many change efforts are disappointing. The following list of causes is compiled from discussions with veteran internal consultants:

- Becoming enamored with the process and forgetting the business
- Skills and tools not matching the concepts being advocated, such as not enough emphasis on statistics
- Lack of leadership and personal involvement by senior managers
- Focusing on reaching a goal or prize without changing the culture
- Trying to do too much at once
- Lack of specific change objectives tied to key business outcomes
- New activities not being mainstreamed into the formal systems

"If you don't know where you are going, any plan will get you there."

145

- Lack of recognition, celebration, and reward
- Bad execution of the plan, or not having a clear plan

One reason for the failure of many change efforts, particularly in total quality management and continuous improvement, is that the efforts have not been linked to the core planning processes of the business. To be successful, a change effort must be a logical extension of the business plan. A change effort should shape the future described by the business plan. A change effort should help the organization align its efforts and improve both planning and execution.

Now let's look at what makes a successful change initiative. Again, the list is based on discussions with experienced consultants. Success factors for organizational change include:

- A clear case for action exists, based on external and internal analysis.
- The change has business relevance, that is, the plan is designed to help realize business goals.
- The implementation approach is sufficient to achieve goals.
- The plan is an output of the organization's formal planning process.
- There are clear roles, detailed plans, and milestones to measure effectiveness.

Building Change Into Business Plans

Applying quality concepts to the planning process is essential for connecting change efforts to business plans. The first step is to recognize that planning is a process that must be continuously improved. In many organizations, planning is done haphazardly and differently every year. People say, "Why

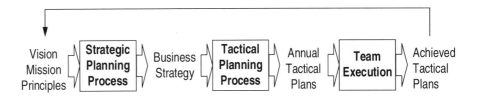

Figure 5.1 High-level Map of the Planning Process

"In planning, it is easy to overestimate what can be accomplished in the short run, and grossly underestimate what can be accomplished in the long run."

bother recording the process, we'll do it differently next year anyway." Planning should be defined as a series of processes with inputs and outputs (see Figure 5.1). Developing a high-level map of the planning process, with feedback loops linking execution back to strategic thinking, provides a foundation for better planning.

Planning should not be an activity driven by number-crunching that multiplies current volume and profitability numbers by desired growth rates and then passes out annual goals. "We should grow volume at 5% and profit at 12% because...we should," the thinking goes. Planning should be based on facts from outside and inside the organization. From the outside should come observations of challenges and opportunities. From the inside should come a data-based understanding of current process capability. The challenge of strategy is to match capability to opportunity and to build new capability to respond to new opportunities and challenges.

Three Phases Of Business Planning

To provide a context for planning for change, let's review the basics of effective business planning. The three phases of business planning are strategic planning, tactical planning, and team execution.

Phase One: The Strategic Planning Process

Strategy begins with the development of a vision, mission and guiding principles. Strategy is defining the most effective path to reach them.

Defining vision, mission, and principles. Envisioning the future is the initial spark in the planning process. The vision is the "why" of planning. The vision describes what the organization wants to be.

"Change everything, except your loves."
Voltaire,
French author

The mission statement describes the accomplishments that will move the organization toward the vision. The mission statement should answer these questions: What are we in business to accomplish? What specific accomplishments will pave the path toward our vision?

Principles are the foundation of common beliefs that will guide the decisions and choices on the road toward the vision. Principles are the beliefs that the company will need to reach the vision, execute the strategy, and inspire the best performance in people.

Defining strategy. Strategy is matching organizational capability with external opportunities to move the organization toward its vision. Opportunity assessment, process capability analysis, and organizational assessment are the activities that produce the three outputs of strategic planning: 1) strategic goals, 2) strategic initiatives, and 3) organization development initiatives. These three outputs make up the business strategy.

"Outside-in" thinking. The strategic thinking process starts with an opportunity assessment. The outside-in planning worksheet in Figure 5.2 offers a simple method of cataloguing emerging trends and factors. New patterns and trends may mean opportunity. Ignoring emerging trends is the fastest way to go out of business. Opportunities are then translated into strategic goals. Strategic goals are the quantitative levels of performance that are essential for the organization to reach its mission and vision. Strategic goals should be written with a time horizon of three to five years. Strategic goals make the mission quantitative and time-bound. They state desired performance in terms of

Opportunity Analysis ➡ Strategic Goals
"Outside-in Thinking"

	Observation	Opportunity
Markets		
Customers		
Technology		
Social		
Government		
Trends		

Figure 5.2 An "Outside-in" Planning Worksheet

growth, profitability, customer and market position, technological superiority, and customer service.

"Inside-out" thinking. The next step is to assess the capability of the processes of the organization. Capability analysis identifies core business processes and quantifies their performance capabilities. To do this effectively, it is important to view the organization as a series of macro work processes. Most organizations can be conceptualized as a handful of processes, such as customer ordering, delivery, manufacturing, product service, and customer service. It may be helpful to draw a macro process model of your organization to define these processes. The model in Figure 5.3 is a sample of a simple process model of an organization.

A quality mindset asks us to evaluate our processes in four dimensions: cost, quality, speed, and customer satisfaction. The worksheet in Figure 5.4

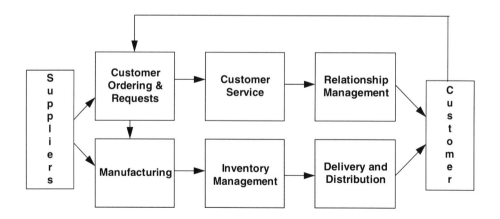

Figure 5.3 A Macro Process Model of an Organization

offers a framework for analysis of a process in terms of its current strengths, and its current gaps, in performance — or the new requirements that customers or the company will place on the process in the future. Discussion about capability should answer the following questions:

- Where would improvements in cost, quality, speed or customer satisfaction provide the greatest competitive advantage for the company?

- How can we leverage what we do well to satisfy the requirements of our customers and capitalize upon the opportunities in the marketplace?

- What gaps exist between what we are promising to our customers today

Capability Analysis ➡ Strategic Initiatives

*Process:*_____   *"Inside-out Thinking"*

	Current Strengths	Current Gaps	New Requirements
Cost			
Quality			
Speed			
Customer Satisfaction			

Figure 5.4 An "Inside-out" Planning Worksheet

and our actual performance?

- Which gaps must be closed now to avoid erosion of our customer base?
- What new requirements must we meet to satisfy emerging needs?
- What new processes must we design in order to be able to develop new products and satisfy unstated future needs of our current and future customers?
- What are we unable to do today, that if we could, would give us a great advantage over our competition?

The priorities for process improvement or process development become strategic initiatives. The initiatives are complete when the capability of the processes is sufficient to achieve the strategic goals.

Optimum organizational structure, systems, culture, and skills. The final step in strategic planning is to envision the kind of organization that can execute the strategy. The organization's principles guide this aspect of planning. Used well, principles can be instruments of change. Principles should be specific and directional. For example, principles should say something about the nature of organization that works best. A principle like, "Management should only add value that customers are willing to pay for," has great implications. Living by this principle would lead you to examine the role and value of managers. A picture of a self-managed organization may begin to emerge. Principles should force debate on distinct choices about the blueprint of the organization.

In addition, the process approach suggests a dramatically different organizational architecture than the functional ones bequeathed to us. An organization should be designed to support its customers and processes. A process-based configuration is likely to be completely different than a functionally-based one. Likewise, there are significant implications for the skills required to operate processes optimally.

Phase Two: The Tactical Planning Process

Strategic planning transforms the organization's vision, mission, and principles into strategic goals (business opportunities), strategic initiatives (process capability development), and organization initiatives (organizational development). Tactical planning transforms this high-level, three-to-five-year thinking into annual objectives. There are three types of objectives:

Business performance objectives. Business performance objectives define the annual business results required to achieve the strategic goals. Examples would be objectives for profitability, market share, and customer satisfaction.

Process capability objectives. Process capability objectives set objectives for process development, process improvement, and process reengineering. These are the infrastructure-building objectives that translate strategic initiatives into specific objectives for improving capability.

Organizational development objectives. Organizational development objectives establish the "software" that drives the organization's "hardware," that is, its work processes. Objectives should be set for the overall architecture of the organization, including the structure, systems, and skills necessary to create the desired culture.

Planning at every level. While strategic planning is primarily the task of senior managers, tactical planning should occur at every level. Tactical planning must occur at four levels of the organization: the whole organization, the business unit, the process ownership group, and the operating team.

Whole organization. The role of the organization leadership team is to test for the sufficiency of the objectives set by the business units to deliver the strategic goals, strategic initiatives, and organizational initiatives.

Business unit. The tactical planning role of the business unit is to set objectives in all categories. Business performance objectives must match current capability. Process capability objectives must build the capability required by the strategy. Organizational development objectives define the necessary systems, structure, and skills.

Process ownership group. Business performance objectives are set for all related processes owned by the process ownership group. For example, a process ownership group representing manufacturing and service processes would set objectives for these processes. Process capability objectives are set for processes that should be redesigned. Organizational development objectives are set to improve structure, systems, and skills.

Team. At the team level, business performance objectives are set to meet the present requirements of internal or external customers. Process capability objectives identify improvement targets for the processes operated by the team. Organizational development objectives concentrate on the immediate skill requirements of the team.

Phase Three: Team Execution

The final phase of planning translates objectives into team action plans and defines a management process to assure that the plans are executed. A team management process assures that daily action is connected to the strategic and tactical plans, and that improvement activities build new capability.

The continuous improvement, or PDEI, cycle is an effective model for team management (see Figure 2.1 in Chapter 2). PDEI describes a sequence of team activities beginning with a performance promise and continuing through improvement activities. The team's objectives are connected to the company's mission and strategy, and represent its unique performance promise to its customers. The three categories of activity that follow the performance promise — deliver, evaluate and improve — are the elements of the team's ongoing self-management process.

The Performance promise. Thinking of your objectives as your performance promise is powerful. Delivering on a performance promise is the most fundamental and tangible definition of competitive advantage. It begins with each individual and team "doing what they say they will do." Objectives that are written according to the TRACC model define the performance promise of the team.

The TRACC model ensures well-written objectives. Check that objectives are:

T — Time-based

R — Reconciled both vertically and horizontally

A — Action-oriented and achievable

C — Written in concise language without vague modifiers like "significantly"

C — Can be counted or measured to judge accomplishment

The format for writing objectives is:

To + action verb + measurable output + level of achievement + time frame.

For example:

To increase the percent of customer requests answered with 24 hours from 75% to 90% by June 30.

The type of objective (business performance objective, process capability objective, or organizational development objective) and the level of the objective (business unit, business ownership group, or team) should be noted.

Deliver on the promise. Quality and customer service are defined by the match between promise and action. Delivering on promises gives integrity to the customer-supplier relationship. To ensure delivery, each type of objective should have a unique kind of action plan.

Business performance objectives. Action plans for business performance objectives tap into current capability. These action plans can be as straightforward as determining what the team needs to do better.

Capability improvement objectives. Action plans for capability improvement objectives cannot be developed by a single operating team. They should be assigned to Process Improvement Teams, or PITs, that cut across functional boundaries.

Organizational development objectives. Individual operating teams build action plans for organizational development objectives. These action plans define how the team will build the skills of the members to operate processes more effectively.

Evaluate progress against the promise. A team should regularly evaluate the match between its performance promises and its delivery. Evaluation requires a set of team measures. A simple but important check is to make sure that the team has measures for each of its objectives. Surprisingly, often a team's objectives and measures don't match. Activities for the team are to:

- Determine a method of measurement for each objective.
- Establish interim goals that assure regular progress toward the objective.
- Identify measures of process performance that serve as "leading indicators" of the status of each objective.
- Evaluate progress at regular team meetings and adjust action plans.

Improve the delivery...and the promise. The final step in the PDEI cycle is to make improvements in the process. "Improvement" used here does not refer to the large-scale improvement in the capability improvement objectives. Here, improvement refers to the continuous, small-scale modifications that occur as a team looks at its performance, addresses its problems, and drives waste and non-value-adding work from its processes.

Implementation Planning

Effective implementation planning includes using some basic planning tools to determine key activities, ownership, and timing. It also involves establishing ways of record keeping, reviewing and reporting progress, and interacting with a steering team.

The nature of implementation planning is affected by whether a new change effort is being rolled out or an existing effort is being refined. In a roll-out, a consultant approaches a unit of the organization and says, in effect, "You need this." In a refinement, the consultant asks the unit, in effect, "What do you need?" A consultant in a long-term client relationship is likely to do both — roll out a series of initiatives in the context of ongoing refinement. Before looking at planning tools, let's look at roll-outs and refinements in more detail.

Roll-out Or Refinement?

Are you planning to kickoff an initial implementation or are you helping your clients maintain and refine a change in progress? A roll-out usually occurs at the beginning of a change effort. A refinement is the ongoing effort to maintain the change and integrate it into everyday life. The two kinds of efforts differ in four specific areas: the scope of the effort, the degree of proactivity required of the consultant, the accountabilities of the consultant and client, and the body of knowledge of the approach being implemented. Figure 5.5 illustrates the key differences between roll-outs and refinements.

Scope Of The Effort

Roll-outs and refinements usually differ in scope. Scope refers to the size and boundaries of the consulting assignment. In a roll-out, you normally have one primary client, the leader of the organization, and your consulting applies to the whole organization. In a refinement, you usually have many clients and your assignments vary from unit to unit in the organization. In a refinement, you normally contract your consulting services with each individual team, your services depend upon the needs and requests of each client, and your time is not likely to be divided evenly among the clients.

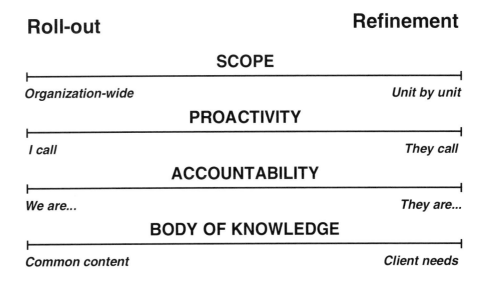

Figure 5.5 Differences Between Roll-outs and Refinements

Proactivity

Proactivity refers to whether you or your client initiates the consulting assignment. How proactive or reactive is your consulting? Do you seek out your clients with a prescribed service or do you wait for them to request your assistance? In a roll-out, the consultant is typically proactive, approaching the client with a change initiative that is occurring throughout the organization. In a refinement, the consultant is usually reactive to the requests of the client. Although the consultant may market his or her services, the client usually chooses when and if to request help from the consultant.

Accountability

Accountability refers to the responsibilities for success of the consultant and client. What is your accountability as a consultant? In a roll-out, the consultant and client are typically both accountable. If a roll-out stalls, the consultant "looks bad" for not taking a more active role in starting it up, and the client "looks bad" for not being more cooperative. In a refinement, it is usually up to the client to make progress. The consultant fulfills his or her accountability by being available and able to help.

Body Of Knowledge

Body of knowledge refers to the content of the consulting services. In a roll-out, the content is usually consistent, with everyone in the organization embracing the same concepts, principles, and skills. There is usually a set body of material that serves as the philosophical and technical basis of the change. In a refinement, the content usually varies according to the requests of the client.

Realizing whether you are consulting in a roll-out, refinement, or a combination of both, and discussing issues of scope, proactivity, accountability, and body of knowledge with your clients can clarify both planning and contracting.

Planning Tools

Basic tools for planning change include planning matrices, Gantt charts, force-field diagrams, and fishbone diagrams.

Planning Matrices

A planning matrix shows the sequence of steps in an implementation and who will be responsible for them. In the planning matrix in Figure 5.6, the implementation steps have been divided into seven sections: Discovery, Leadership, Preparation, Awareness, Skill Development, Implementation, and Systems Redesign. Discovery is building the knowledge base about the change initiative. Leadership is what the leaders do to prepare for the change. Preparation develops the skills of the change agents. Awareness is the communication that announces the reasons for the change. Skill Development is the training that everyone receives. Implementation is putting the change into practice. Systems Redesign is the modification of systems, processes, and policies to support the change. The matrix shows four groups that will take action: the senior team, a quality council, the internal consultants, and the operating teams themselves. (In this case, "quality council" refers to an implementation steering group that includes members of the senior team, representatives from a "diagonal slice" of the organization, and the internal consultants). The matrix also labels the responsibility of each group at each

Continuous Improvement Planning Matrix	☑ primary responsibility ✓ participates ⇧ assists	Senior Team	Quality Council	Internal Consultants	Teams
DISCOVERY					
Learn from model companies		✓	☑	⇧	
Visit successful companies		✓	☑	⇧	
Assess the competitive position of the company		☑	✓	⇧	
PLANNING					
Define the current state and end state		☑	✓	⇧	
Establish concrete improvement goals		☑	✓	⇧	
Determine methods of measurement for the initiative		☑	✓	⇧	
Develop an implementation plan and time frame		☑	✓	⇧	
Form strategic partnership with external change agent		☑	✓	⇧	
LEADERSHIP					
Establish a vision, mission and guiding principles		☑	✓	⇧	
Develop a communication and listening plan		✓	☑	⇧	
Assess the current organizational configuration		☑	✓	⇧	
Document the strategic significance of the initiative		☑	✓	⇧	
Behavioralize the practices required by the strategy		✓	✓	☑	
Link the initiative to key business results		☑	✓	⇧	
Identify macro processes critical to success		☑	✓	⇧	
PREPARATION					
Pick the best and brightest for internal consulting team		☑	✓		
Train internal consultants extensively				☑	
AWARENESS					
Publicize the initiative on an ongoing basis		✓	☑	⇧	✓
Hold awareness sessions about the initiative		☑	✓	⇧	✓
SKILL BUILDING					
Train teams in process improvement skills		✓	✓	☑	✓
Train teams in the tools of quality		✓	✓	☑	✓
Train teams in team effectiveness skills		✓	✓	☑	✓
IMPLEMENTATION					
Identify key processes for improvement		☑	✓	⇧	☑
Identify customer requirements and receive feedback		☑	✓	⇧	☑
Communicate requirements and feedback to suppliers		☑	✓	⇧	☑
Define and track measures of team performance		☑	✓	⇧	☑
Conduct regular team meetings		☑	✓	⇧	☑
SUPPORT SYSTEMS REDESIGN					
Identify opportunities for system and policy changes		✓	☑	⇧	✓
Implement system and policy changes		☑	✓	⇧	✓

Figure 5.6 A Planning Matrix Showing Responsibilities at Each Step

step as "owns," "participates," and "assists." The group that "owns" the step must initiate it and drive it to completion. The group that "participates" in a step can expect to be involved and give input. The group that "assists" in a step can expect to facilitate or provide other help.

Figure 5.7 is another example of a planning matrix, in this case showing the relationships among training, team action, and consulting follow-up in a 14-step implementation. In this example, the 14 steps refer to the 14 chapters in *Continuous Improvement: Teams & Tools.*

Senior Team Vision & Training   **Implementation Planning**

Training for Team Action →	Team Action ←	Coaching on Team Action
1. Paradigms for Improvement	Describe applicability to the team	One-to-one discussion & facilitate groups
2. The PDEI Cycle	Identify company's performance promise	Help apply at the team level
3. Leadership Requirement	Discuss leaders' vision and principles	Help identify gap between today & future
4. Team Charter	Create team charter	Give examples and help edit
5. Process Management	Analyze key processes, redesign	Facilitate process analysis sessions
6. Measurement	Identify process measures, scorecard	Offer examples, check across teams
7. Team Development	Team assesses itself	Facilitate team building
8. Communication	Apply skills to team discussions	Observe and give feedback
9. Team Effectiveness	Hold regular team meetings	Prep, observe, give feedback
10. Problem Solving	Apply techniques to team processes	Coach, facilitate, give feedback
11. Fundamentals of SPC	Apply tools of SPC to team processes	Coach, suggest, give examples
12. Team Decision Making	Clarify authorities and involvement	Help identify key decisions & facilitate
13. Advanced Teams	Develop plan to mature to next level	Offer observations and suggestions
14. Self Management	Develop personal improvement plans	Coach, suggest, help define specifics

Other Topics... →   **Continued Action** ←   **Continued Coaching**

Figure 5.7 A Planning Matrix Showing the Relationships Among Training, Team Action, and Consulting Follow-up

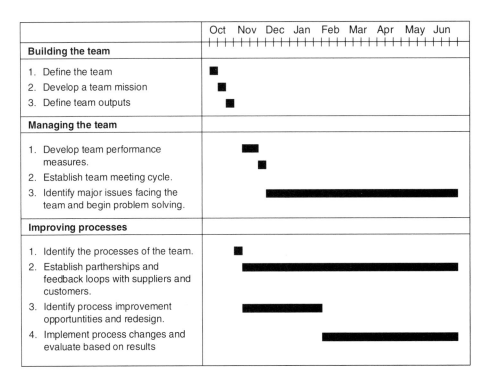

	Oct	Nov	Dec	Jan	Feb	Mar	Apr	May	Jun
Building the team									
1. Define the team									
2. Develop a team mission									
3. Define team outputs									
Managing the team									
1. Develop team performance measures.									
2. Establish team meeting cycle.									
3. Identify major issues facing the team and begin problem solving.									
Improving processes									
1. Identify the processes of the team.									
2. Establish partherships and feedback loops with suppliers and customers.									
3. Identify process improvement opportunties and redesign.									
4. Implement process changes and evaluate based on results									

Figure 5.8 A Gantt Chart

Gantt Charts

A Gantt chart is designed to show the relationships in time among implementation steps, and to compare the rates of planned versus actual progress. To construct a Gantt chart, list the steps in the implementation in a column and extend the timeline (usually in weeks) across the top of the chart. Draw bars to indicate the starting point, duration, and stopping point of each step. Figure 5.8 shows a nine-month Gantt chart for a team's participation in the implementation of a team management system.

Driving Forces ⟶	⟵ Restraining Forces
• Awareness of the changing industry and the changing lifestyles of customers and employees.	• Negative experiences with empowerment in the past.
• The human resource is getting more competitive and costly.	• Positive experiences with tight control in the past.
• The change is in-line with company values.	• The new activities take time, which is scarce in the organization.
• The training is known to be effective.	• The payback on the change will be long-term rather than short-term.
• The commitment to change exists both at the top and at the front line.	• Some new behaviors go against the behaviors that have made the company successful in the past.
• New technology is available to support the change.	• The change effort does not "feel" like it's going to produce results.
• Customers are demanding changes.	• The change effort tends to talk about how's, not about results.
• Competitors are also changing.	
• Need to communicate continuously about the change.	• Fear of the unknown in the organization.
• Need to get some early successes.	• Fear of "getting shot down."
• Need to coach senior managers on new behaviors.	• Resistance to measuring performance.
• Need to focus on business results.	

Figure 5.9 A Force-field Diagram

Force-field Diagrams

A force-field diagram (see Chapter 3) shows the driving forces propelling an implementation toward successful completion and the restraining forces inhibiting it. A force-field diagram lists all existing drivers and restrainers and draws them in opposition. A force-field diagram is a useful tool for facilitating discussion between the consultant and client about the strength of existing drivers and restrainers, how additional drivers can be added, and how existing restrainers can be neutralized or overcome. The force-field diagram in Figure 5.9 shows a list of driving and restraining forces at the start of a total quality management implementation.

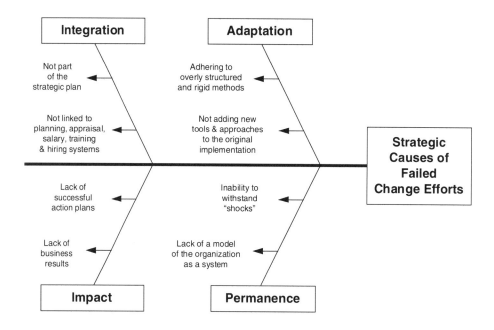

Figure 5.10 Fishbone Diagram of Strategic Causes of Failed Change

Fishbone Diagrams

Fishbone diagrams can be used to identify possible causes of failure and plan for their prevention. A fishbone diagram is a way of capturing and organizing possible causes of implementation problems: "What if it's two years from now and this change never took hold. What might have happened to cause this?" The items are intentionally written in negative terms. The leaders and consultants want to prevent these factors from occurring during the implementation.

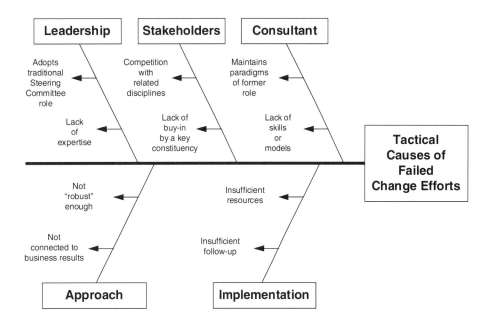

Figure 5.11 Fishbone Diagram of Tactical Causes of Failed Change

The fishbone diagram in Figure 5.10 shows possible *strategic* causes of failed change. Strategic failure refers to the "big-picture" ways a change can fail. In the diagram, the category labeled "Integration" refers to whether the change is "built into" the everyday workings of the organization. The change effort should be linked to planning, appraisal, salary, training, and hiring systems. "Adaptation" refers to whether the tools and methods of the change initiative are continually improved, added to, and made as practical and easy-to-use as possible. "Impact" refers to whether there are successful action plans and improved results. "Permanence" refers to whether the change initiative can withstand "shocks," such as a business downturn, and whether the change has a significant impact on the organization as an overall system.

The fishbone diagram in Figure 5.11 shows possible *tactical* causes of failed change. Tactical failure refers to the "nitty-gritty, real-world" ways a change can fail. "Leadership" refers to whether the leaders understand and execute their roles. Rather than simply reviewing the progress of the change agents (in the manner of a traditional steering committee), the senior team must counsel, communicate, and coordinate. Leaders should also develop real expertise in the content of the change initiative. "Stakeholders" refers to the degree of buy-in by key constituencies and degree of competition among the related disciplines involved in the change. The category of "Consultant" refers to how well the consultant executes his or her role. The consultant must have the time, skills, and conceptual models to implement the change. "Approach" refers to whether the initiative is "robust" enough to produce change and whether it is connected to business results. "Implementation" refers to how the initiative is managed and executed. Resources and follow-up must be sufficient to support the plan.

Record-Keeping And Reporting

Consultants should keep records of each consulting contact and each team or individual's action plan related to the change effort. The consultant must keep sufficient records to answer the questions: "What did we discuss in our last contact and what were the action steps? and "What is the client working on?" Assume that your clients expect professional record-keeping similar to what you expect by your physician, dentist, or accountant.

In most change efforts, the participants are expected to maintain the detailed information related to their participation in the change effort. For example, in the implementation of a team management system, the teams themselves should keep copies of team action plans, team meeting agendas and team action records, team graphs and charts, team meeting feedback sheets, customer feedback, and feedback to suppliers.

The consultant's monthly report to the top client and Steering Team should describe: activities completed, feedback from the teams, "good news" and current challenges, and desired Steering Team action. An outline for reporting on progress, either in written or spoken form, is:

- Review the plan. "According to our plan, what should be accomplished at this point is..."
- Report steps accomplished and results. "What we have actually accomplished is..."
- Recount positive events and examples. "Some things that we feel good about are..."
- Issues and concerns. "Some issues that we feel have to be addressed are..."
- Outline the Internal Consultants' next steps. "The next steps we are taking are..."
- Outline the Senior Team's next steps. "What we'd like to ask you to do is..."

Steering Teams

The purpose of a Steering Team is to develop and manage an evolving plan for change and assure that the change initiative is connected to the business. Rather than simply review and evaluate the work of the consultants, the Steering Team should assume ownership and responsibility for success.

The membership of the Steering Team should include the senior team, representatives of key stakeholders (such as unions), and representatives from a "diagonal slice" of the organization. The Steering Team should meet monthly to guide the implementation. Steering teams have three basic roles: counseling, communicating, and coordinating.

Counseling. Counseling refers to selecting and adapting the best approach, identifying boundaries, making decisions, and providing resources. The Steering Team should review the data collected by the consultant on the progress of the change effort (see Chapter 4). Is the change effort progressing? What issues and concerns are being raised by the consultant? What issues are being raised by the members of the organization? What decisions or choices must be made at this stage of the implementation? What additional resources, such as time, information, or expertise, are needed in the change effort? Where is leadership action currently required?

Communicating. Communicating includes creating a vision, managing communication, modeling behavior, and communicating with customers. The Steering Team should determine what new messages should be communicated about the change, what questions must be answered, and what confusions must be clarified. Is the change effort visible enough in the organization? Is the leaders' support of the change apparent to the members? Where should new communication links with customers or suppliers or within the organization be formed?

Coordinating. Coordinating refers to managing the change effort at a high level. Coordinating includes connecting the change effort to the business, benchmarking and setting goals for change, maintaining long-term focus, integrating improvement efforts, identifying systems to be changed, preventing suboptimization, and managing reward and recognition.

Gathering Support For The Plan

The most common complaint of change agents is lack of sufficient management support. Part of planning is assessing and managing the levels of support among the stakeholders of the change effort.

Stakeholder Analysis: The House Of Commitment

An effective way of identifying support among stakeholders of the change is to construct a House of Commitment. A House of Commitment is a planning matrix in which the stakeholders are analyzed in terms of their accountabilities, aspirations, circumstances, and receptivity.

The first step in constructing a House of Commitment is to identify the key stakeholders in the change. Key stakeholders include the "Organizational Owner" and "Organizational Subowners," "Champions" and "Stars," and "Related Disciplines." The "Organizational Owner" is your top client, the leader of the part of the organization to which you are consulting. The "Organizational Subowners" are the direct reports of the Organizational Owner. "Champions" are those who are already outspoken supporters of the change. "Stars" are individuals who are ready to implement the change, thus serving as role models and providing success stories. "Related Disciplines" are other change agents and staff groups who might be allies or competitors for the time, attention, and resources of the your clients. To collaborate with these related disciplines, it is important to understand their goals and motives.

Next, for each stakeholder, ask yourself what you know about that person's goals, motives, and receptivity. Divide your analysis into four areas: accountability, aspirations, circumstance, and receptivity.

Accountability

"Accountability" refers to the stakeholder's performance promise. What business results has the stakeholder committed to? What are his or her deliverables? In particular, which of the stakeholder's performance commitments are likely to be affected by the change? Will the change help revenue grow? Will the change produce a decrease in cost or error? Will the change produce greater efficiency? Understanding the stakeholder's accountability helps the consultant predict his or her interest in the change.

Aspirations

"Aspirations" refer to the personal motivations of the stakeholder with regard to the change. From a personal perspective, what does the stakeholder want? What's a win for this person? What are his or her personal desires and how do they relate to the change? Does the stakeholder want to be promoted? Does the stakeholder want to look good in front of peers? Does he or she want to leave a positive change as a legacy to the organization? Does the stakeholder want to make the organization a better place? Does the person want to finish out this job assignment without minimal stress and strain? Does the person want to avoid a long-term change effort in favor of short-term operational results? Understanding the stakeholder's aspirations will help the consultant "position" the change effort appropriately and persuasively.

Circumstance

"Circumstance" refers to the challenge faced by the stakeholder. In what condition is this stakeholder? Does the person have a goal that he or she wants to (or must) attain? Does the person have a problem that he or she must solve?

	Accountability (business)	Aspirations (personal)	Circumstance (goal, problem or OK?)	Receptivity (-3 to +3)
Organizational Owner Bill Anderson	Performance indicators in the business plan? ■	Leave a legacy of a great culture	Problem: Improve customer satisfaction? ■	+3: Has seen it work in other places
Organizational Subowners Bev Johnson	Performance indicators? ■	Is a believer and would like to implement it	Problem: Control costs	+3: Likes the philosophy
Paul Martinez	Performance indicators? ■	Look good on short-term #'s ■	OK: Feels no need to change	-2: Sees it as disruptive fad ■
Anna Lee	Performance indicators? ■	Would like more people ■	Problem: Missed deadlines ■	0: Not focused on it ■
Champions & Stars Mary Blake	Call center performance goals	Wants to stop the fire-fighting	Problem: Currently below goals	+3: Ready to begin training
Peter McBain	On-time installation goals	Meet B. Anderson expectations	Goal: Would like "breakthrough"	+3: Asking for consulting help
Doug Peterson	Response time to customer requests	Look promotable in the new culture	Problem: Negative customer feedback	+3: Ready to try anything
Related Disciplines Ed Jones (Trg)	Training goals? ■	Be part of the change	Problem: "Sell" trg to line org? ■	+1: Positive, somewhat familiar
Tim Evans (HR)	HR goals? Change goals? ■	Coordinate all change work? ■	Goal: Redefine HR services? ■	+2: Positive, some experience

Figure 5.12 A House of Commitment

Or, is the person currently without goals or problems and, in fact, comfortable with the status quo? In other words, is the person at the foot of a mountain, in a hole, or on a flat plain? As change agents, we would like stakeholders to have a goal to accomplish or a problem to solve. A stakeholder with no problem or goal, who is in a comfortable circumstance, is likely to find the effort of change an unnecessary expense.

Receptivity

"Receptivity" refers to the stakeholder's present view of the change initiative itself. Does the person view it in a positive light? Is the person a "believer"? Does the person see it as a way to meet his or her accountabilities, fulfill his or her aspirations, and address his or her condition?

Think of the matrix as a house and each cell as a door. For each cell, is the door open or closed? The door is open if you know the answer to the question represented by that cell, and the answer is positive to the change effort. Draw an open rectangle to signify that the door is open to you as a change agent. The door is currently closed if you don't know where the person stands on this question, or if the answer is bad news. In that case, draw a shaded rectangle to indicate a closed door. Figure 5.12 shows an example of a completed House of Commitment. You should not be surprised to find a large number of closed doors. You must figure out how to open each closed door. How can you find out more about this stakeholder? Who's going to "knock on that door"? You may simply ask the person, or ask a champion or star who knows that person to "open the door" for you.

Those whose accountabilities and aspirations present a goal or problem, and who are receptive to the change initiative, will "open the door" the soonest. Those who are comfortable in terms of their accountabilities and aspirations, or who don't see the change effort as valuable, will be slow to respond. If the person "answers the door," but the answer isn't favorable, the consultant must coach, persuade, or confront the person (see Chapter 3), or get the needed support by "going through another door," in other words, by talking to another stakeholder.

Summary

In this chapter, we have described how to connect the change effort to the business planning of the organization, how to plan the implementation itself, and how to assess the existing levels of support among the stakeholders. In the next chapter, we will look at Contracting, the next step in the consulting cycle, in detail.

Addendum A: Guidelines For Leading Change

Leaders must provide true leadership for large-scale organizational change to be successful. Guiding change effectively is one of the important jobs of leaders in a world that knows change as its only constant.

To lead change, you have to change. If the organization is nothing more, or less, than a collection of individuals, then organizational transformation is born of personal transformation. Organizational transformation is accompanied by, and caused by, personal transformation. No personal transformation is more important than that of the leaders. The ten points that follow are intended to help leaders think about what will be required if they are to negotiate the tortuous road of change successfully.

1. Fire in the belly. Don't put your organization through a profound change unless you have steeled yourself for the effort and have a passionate conviction about the necessity for, and value of, change. Think about what the organization will need to be like five and ten years from now to be successful. Your vision must reflect passion and urgency for change. It must describe a future that has benefits strong enough to pull an organization through the tough work to come. Your task is to create a compelling case for action in your own mind before going further. Don't risk your organization or cause the pain of changing to be part of a fad.

2. Honest self-assessment. Vaughn Beals of Harley-Davidson noted that all of their efforts to revitalize Harley were unsuccessful until the leaders said, "The problem is us." To lead change, you must see yourself as you are seen by the followers in your organization. The trouble is that leaders are usually the last people in the organization to hear honest feedback. If you don't know how the leadership team is perceived, find out. Conduct a survey to feel the pulse of the people and learn how the organization as a whole, and the leadership team in particular, are perceived.

3. Balance time and priorities. Leaders signal the importance of initiatives by how they spend their time. The problem is that there are too many ways to spend leadership time that are all "right." No one will challenge how leaders spend their time, so the senior team must establish the strategic priority of the quality initiative and define how each member of the team will spend time to support the effort. Some general suggestions about how to spend time are:

- Spend at least one quarter of your time with customers.
- Spend at least one quarter of your time with people at least two levels removed from your team. This should include significant time with frontline employees who deal with customers every day.
- Spend more time listening to the organization than communicating your message about the direction and performance goals of the company.
- Spend 10% of your time learning the skills and tools of continuous improvement.
- Demonstrate through your actions that the surest way to see immediate improvement and long term results is through the application of continuous improvement practices.

4. Model the principles. The tools of quality and continuous improvement are straightforward and can be mastered from the shop floor to the executive tower. The tools have their greatest value when they are applied in an environment that has adopted a new paradigm for managing. Guiding principles articulate this new paradigm and leaders have the job of making the new paradigm real. Principles are the rock-solid tenets that all employees can count on. They offer security and confidence by making leadership behavior predictable. Demonstrate the validity of the principles, when they are developed, by showing how they guide the tough decisions.

5. Incorporate within your strategic framework. A quality or continuous improvement effort should be part of the overall strategic plan for the organization. This plan must be integrated into the fabric of the organization and must be real for associates at every level. The best way to make it real is to mainstream the process into the planning and objective-setting process.

6. Understand the dynamics of change. The diagram below describes the important dynamics of change. Leaders must be aware of the learning curves, intellectual and habitual, and the accompanying emotional stages the people of your organization will experience.

The curve of intellectual knowledge occurs as a result of training and moves up the change axis quickly. The habit change curve moves up the change axis much more slowly. The distance between what has been learned intellectually and what is practiced habitually represents the change gap. Everyone has probably experienced the discomfort that this gap brings. In tennis, for instance, one can be an intellectual champion commenting expertly on every situation and shot, while being unable to execute any of the shots on the court. Change is successful when ideas and information have been translated into enduring habits.

There are very predictable emotional stages that accompany learning and change (see Figure 5.13). Change always initiates excitement or fear at the outset. We have all experienced the combined emotions of elation, "Great, I got the job," followed by fear, "Oh no, how am I going to do that job?"

The second stage of change is the most difficult. At the point when

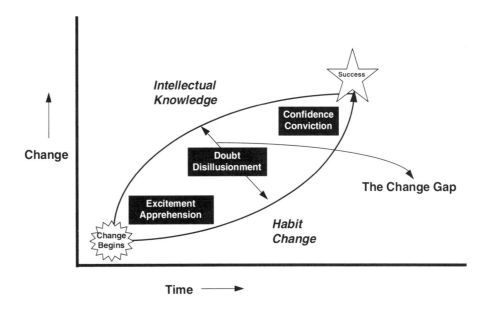

Figure 5.13 The Dynamics of Change

learning is greatest, the learner has also become painfully aware of the gap between what is in the book and what is in the habits. Many feel doubt and even disillusionment at this point. This is like week two of a diet: you know what has to be done and you also know just how hard it will be to reach the goal. This is a stage that must be traversed because awareness of the gap between what you want, and where you are, is the catalyst for fundamental change.

In the final stage, positive emotions accompany the rapidly growing habit curve. This is the fun and easy part of change. New skills are working and broad applications are being discovered.

Every individual and every team will go through the curve at a different pace. People will be at different stages throughout the change effort. Those who have confidence in their use of new skills and ideas will often be intolerant of those who are working through periods of doubt. Helpful leadership will provide empathy, coaching, and reward for effort during this stage.

7. Expect cynicism. Expect cynicism from employees who have been through one too many programs. Cynicism should be anticipated, understood, and used as a source of energy for change. Cynicism comes from cognitive dissonance. Cognitive dissonance describes how we feel when there is imbalance between our stated beliefs and our daily behavior. Individuals seek balance by changing behavior or rationalizing beliefs. Dissonance can be a constructive force for change in an organization when individuals are empowered to help bring about positive change. The practical lessons are:

- Enlist everyone in the change process. Change shouldn't be something that is happening to anyone, but rather, change is a process being brought about by the people of the organization.
- Leaders must reduce unnecessary dissonance by behaving consistently with the vision, mission, and principles.

8. Plan to win with results. The plan to change the culture of an organization must be well thought out and comprehensive. Develop a plan that is designed to win by articulating the important results that should be achieved as the process is implemented. Set improvement goals in the soft category (cultural characteristics) and the hard category (business performance).

A macro plan is essential at the outset, but don't "fall in love" with the plan. Fall in love with the vision and mission, and modify the plan as you learn and as events change. Stay constant about where you are going, and stay flexible about how to get there.

Don't wait for the perfect plan or the perfect time before you begin. Neither has ever existed. Begin with a three-year macro plan that defines the future state and three or four transition states that the organization will move through on its progression toward your vision. Develop detailed training and implementation plans that have a planning horizon of 90 to 180 days. Continue developing these 180-day plans incorporating the knowledge you have gained.

9. Stay externally focused on the customer. Change efforts of this kind often fail because the link between the effort and the purpose of the business is not clear from the outset or becomes vague. Should this linkage deteriorate, the first crisis will push the plan onto the back shelf. Maintain the importance of the effort by staying externally focused and constantly linking the effort to the ultimate customer satisfaction goals of the enterprise. Stay customer-focused by:

- Establishing customer satisfaction and retention as the most important measure of the company.
- Saturating the organization with the voice of the customer.
- Sharing all customer survey data with everyone.
- Copying others on customer feedback.
- Meeting "belly-to-belly" with real customers informally and frequently and sharing observations.

10. Savor the quest. Your vision and principles will make this odyssey a noble quest. As you embark on this voyage, it helps to embrace the philosophy of continuous improvement from the outset and begin to derive satisfaction from the fact that the journey has begun. Each step of progress, each moment of learning from every mistake, can be a source of satisfaction and motivation to continue.

Addendum B: Initial Implementation Checklist

____ 1. Align the goals of the process with the goals of the leaders.

____ 2. Establish contracts with leaders, participants, and other stakeholders.

____ 3. Identify and train internal consultants.

____ 4. Determine the name and logo for the process.

____ 5. Identify office space, supplies, and other physical resources.

____ 6. Identify who is on what team and how many team leaders there will be.

____ 7. Schedule and plan logistics on Kickoff, Orientation Sessions, and Team Training.

____ 8. Identify the content and design of the training.

____ 9. Arrange for correct number of training workbooks.

____ 10. Identify who will do what training.

____ 11. Plan training logistics (rooms, materials, and so forth).

____ 12. Schedule participants for training (names, dates, and announcements).

____ 13. Determine goals and performance indicators of the implementation in terms of what to track, how to track it, how to display it, and what data currently exists.

_____ 14. Decide how to track the progress of the implementation, as well as the performance of the consulting team.

_____ 15. Schedule meetings of the Steering Team.

_____ 16. Determine the need for customer feedback based on what data currently exists, and identify options for collecting additional data.

_____ 17. Decide how to interview people for their views on the change effort.

_____ 18. Set up a record-keeping system for the internal consultants.

_____ 19. Determine the ideal frequency and timing of team meetings.

_____ 20. Plan the frequency of consulting contacts.

_____ 21. Identify potential performance measures for each team.

_____ 22. Develop templates and worksheets for team action plans, problem solving, process analysis, and other activities in the implementation.

_____ 23. Develop a communications plan to inform the members of the organization about the change effort.

_____ 24. Identify and arrange for attention-getting signs, symbols, and "giveaways" to promote and publicize the implementation.

_____ 25. Identify and arrange for recognition and rewards of all types for participation and success in the process.

6

Contracting

6

Contracting

The third step in the consulting cycle is Contracting. Contracting is the step that distinguishes consulting from other types of project and staff work. Contracting ensures that consulting is a collaborative relationship *with* the client, not just a set of tasks done *for* the client.

The objectives of this chapter are to present a model for contracting and guidelines for establishing effective contracts.

What Is Contracting?

Contracting is getting the change effort off on the right foot. In quality language, contracting seeks to prevent the common problems of consulting upfront. Common problems of consulting include:

- The leader is not part of the intervention
- Resources are not sufficient
- The consultants do not have the support of the leaders
- The leaders don't change themselves
- The change activities are not close enough to the business
- The scope of the effort is too large or too small
- The consultant does not have credibility or access to the leader

These problems can and should be prevented through contracting.

Contracting is a set of expectations agreed upon by people working together. The goal of contracting is to establish a mutual set of expectations about what will happen, who will do what, and what is needed for success. Underlying this goal is the understanding that the roles of the leader and consultant during change are interdependent. Very little can happen in a change process unilaterally. This is somewhat different from the supplier-customer model in which the customer states the requirements and the supplier goes about meeting them. For example, as a consultant, I can't begin to coach you unless you agree to let me watch you in action and to accept my observations willingly. You must agree to give access, time, and openness. This is as important as the perceptiveness of my observations and the helpfulness of my suggestions.

Contracting is both a dialogue and a document. The act of discussing expectations and requirements establishes the consulting relationship, sets the stage for future consulting contacts, and surfaces each side's view of critical success factors. Also, contracting can and should produce a document that can serve as a cornerstone of the relationship.

The Benefits Of Contracting

Most consulting failures are failures of contracting. In other words, most consulting problems could have been avoided with a clearer exchange of expectations and requirements for success. Most consulting problems occur because someone didn't know that something was necessary or thought someone else would do it. Contracting thus is beneficial because:

- It clarifies expectations between the leader and the consultant.

- It establishes the implementation as mutual.
- It is the first consulting interaction.
- It establishes an honest relationship without any pretending.

First, plain and simple, contracting specifies what the leader and consultant expect of each other. This sounds straightforward, but it is not. The following are some typical examples of misunderstood expectations.

- The leader expects specific business results to improve, while the consultant expects people to implement action plans of their choosing.
- The leader expects the consultant to take the leadership role in speeches and so forth, while the consultant expects the same of the leader.
- The leader expects the change to come from the people, while the consultant expects the change to start with the leader.
- The leader expects the consultant to know what the key measures should be and where the leverage points are to produce positive results, while the consultant expects guidance on this from the leader.
- The leader expects the change to take a year, while the consultant expects it to take five years.

Second, change requires collaborative action by the leader and change agent, and contracting establishes the change implementation as a partnership, not as a delegation or a directive. If the leader balks at the idea that the change implementation involves requirements on his or her behavior, then the effort was going to have problems shortly anyway.

Third, contracting is really the first consulting interaction. The process of clarifying expectations, sharing observations, making recommendations, giving honest assessments, and identifying needed action steps will be a normal part of consulting. Contracting is really the first consulting contact — the objective of the contact is to define the consultant-client relationship and the expectations for the change effort.

Finally, speaking the truth is the best chance the consultant has to get what he or she wants — the ear of the leader, a collegial relationship, and access to power. The consultant wants to be taken seriously — leaders take people seriously who honestly state what's going on. Consultants want to give input — leaders take input from people who talk about what it will take to be successful. Consultants want to be respected — leaders respect those who give honest opinions. At the same time, speaking the truth is the hardest thing for the consultant. The messages typically sent by the organizational culture are: "Don't rock the boat...Don't let them shoot the messenger...Don't upset powerful people...Don't admit you don't know something...Make things sound better than they are...Say you'll handle everything...Say there's no problem." Thus, contracting can be a tense experience because the consultant must act contrary to cultural messages. The consultant must persevere, accepting that any tension in contracting will only be magnified in the future if differing expectations are not surfaced and clarified.

Why Contracting Does Not Occur

In spite of the benefits listed above, contracting is often a skipped step in the consulting cycle. There are many reasons why contracting doesn't occur:

- The consultant feels most comfortable providing deliverables and wants to get right to it.

- The consultant feels pressure to do something to earn his or her keep.

- The consultant has unrealistic optimism in the power of the deliverables.

- The consultant hopes to "shape" a relationship with the leader over time without having to raise specific issues.

- The consultant wants to "get a foot in the door" or "plant a seed."

- The consultant wants to study the situation more before discussing mutual expectations.

- The consultant is confident that he or she will look good as a result of the deliverables regardless of their overall impact on the client.

- The consultant thinks, "The dynamics of this situation feel strained already, so why bring up more difficult subjects? I better go with the flow."

- The consultant takes the invitation to participate as a signal that expectations are clear.

- The consultant is intimidated by the authority of the leader and uncomfortable expressing needs and requirements.

- The consultant has sold the intervention as "self-contained" without stating the importance of the leader's involvement.

- The consultant is uncomfortable describing his or her less-than-perfect capabilities and so overpromises: "Yes, I can convince all of them to do this without your help."

- The consultant is not exactly sure what will be needed from the leader and so asks for nothing.

- The consultant feels that the leader would consider not being able to make things happen single-handedly as weak or unmotivated.

- The environment is a new one for the consultant and rather than say the wrong thing, he or she waits to understand the culture better.

- The consultant doesn't want to hurt anyone's feelings and raising concerns about competence, capability, or possible failure would do that.
- There are unique aspects to the intervention, such as late involvement or other change agents, that make the consultant overly cautious.

None of these is sufficient reason not to contract!

The Values Required For Contracting

The values underlying contracting are proactivity and authenticity. Proactivity is important because rarely does anyone complain about not getting pinned down on requirements and expectations. It is unusual for a client to say, "You need to push me outside of my comfort zone. I am bound to part of the problem as well. You need to make yourself a significant influence on my behavior, and even though I've delegated this to you, it needs to be a major commitment of my time, energy, and creativity." Many clients are used to working with unspoken or half-spoken expectations. Also, most people expect the professional service-provider to set whatever ground rules are necessary (for example, I expect my accountant to tell me what I must do to document my financial life). The consultant must take the first step in contracting.

The best way to understand contracting is to consider the simplest model of consulting. In this model, there are three entities: the leader, the members of the organization, and the consultant. Initially, the leader is likely to see the change effort as a project and to approach the assignment from a project-delegation paradigm — that is, the leader will expect to give the consultant the mission of providing help to the teams and individuals in the organization. In this view, the leader sees the consultant as a project manager. This is the classic delegation-to-staff model familiar to any manager. Figure 6.1 illustrates this paradigm, with an arrow from the leader to the consultant and one from the consultant to the team or individual.

The change process, however, requires interaction among the three entities. Since the culture of the organization depends so much on the style and behavior of the leader, the consultant will want to influence the leader as well as the participants. Thus, the consultant will want to ask for commitments from the leader. For example, to influence the leader's behavior, the consultant will want access to the leader. Access means letting the consultant observe the

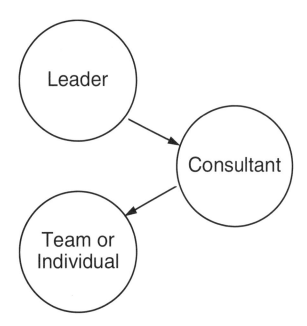

Figure 6.1 The Project-delegation Paradigm

leader in action, give feedback, share observations about the implementation, advise the leader relative to the change effort, see relevant data and plans, and be part of the leader's meetings and other activities. *This is probably not what the leader initially had in mind.*

The consultant would also like the leader to realize that the consulting will be influenced by the feedback of the teams and individuals. Their feedback should affect the behavior of the consultant and the leader. Finally, the consultant would like the leader to provide a sense of vision, excitement, and authority to the participants directly, and be open to the participants' input and feedback.

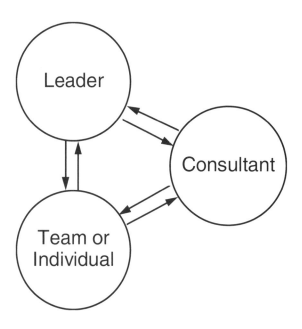

Figure 6.2 The Triadic Model of Consulting

The arrows in Figure 6.2 show these connections among all three entities, forming the triadic model of consulting. These connections are essential to the change process. A change effort is not a typical project, and delegation should not be the defining paradigm of the consultant-client relationship. Contracting seeks to establish a new paradigm in the mind of the leader.

The 7 R's Of An Effective Contract

A consultant-client contract should cover some specific topics. A useful model for the elements of a contract are the "7 R's":

- Results — What we expect to accomplish
- Roadmap — The basic plan we will follow
- Roles — The basic parts each will play in the implementation
- Responsibilities — The expectations and accountabilities of each role
- Resources — What it will take in terms of time, budget, and so forth
- Reporting — How progress will be communicated and reviewed
- Relationship — How we will handle decisions, feedback, and problems

Let's look at each element in detail.

Results

The contract should address the specific desired outcomes of the change effort. What are we aiming to accomplish? What is the objective of the effort? What are the client's criteria for success? What will the client consider "a good job"? How will the consultant and client know if the change effort is not succeeding? What is the scope of the effort? How much of the organization will be involved? Is any policy or system of the organization "out-of-bounds" with regard to the change effort?

Roadmap

What is the overall plan? What are the key interventions, major milestones, and basic time-frames? Who must do what by when to implement the change and accomplish the results? The plan can be described at a high level for the purposes of the contract. Of course, detailed plans are eventually necessary to manage the implementation (see Chapter 5).

Roles

What are the key roles of the consultant and client? The basic roles of the consultant include communications director, trainer, coach, and system designer. The role of coach can be further delineated as advisor, facilitator, data analyst, content expert, implementation partner, or a combination of the above. The basic roles of the leader are: visionary, teacher and learner, manager, and builder of systems. The roles may be further specified as participant, role model, resource provider, communicator, and decision-maker.

Responsibilities

In the context of the defined roles, what specifically are the consultant and client counting on each other to do? An example would be that the consultant's training role will include responsibilities to design and deliver all of the training. Another example would be that the leader's management role will include regular review sessions with direct reports about progress. This is the opportunity for both parties to say specifically what each needs from the other. For example, if the consultant believes that the leader should talk to each team, this should be raised as part of the leader's communication role.

Resources

What people, time, budget, information, skills, and outside help are needed to accomplish the effort? Resources refer to all of the help that might be needed. Resources may include: people's time to work with you, access to information, learning materials, availability of experts in the organization (such as financial people to assist in developing measures), and the use of outside experts or associations.

Reporting

What is the most effective means and frequency for reviewing progress? How often will the client and consultant review the progress of the implementation, the consultant's deliverables, and results to date, as well as identify new action items? Will the reporting be written, spoken, face-to-face, voice mail or e-mail? We strongly suggest that a monthly one-page status report be part of the reporting system (see Chapter 5).

Relationship

How will the consultant and client work together? In what ways will the consultant have access to the client? How will the consultant and client make decisions, exchange feedback, and solve problems? How formal or informal will the relationship be? What will be the primary means of communicating? It is particularly important for the consultant to acknowledge that he or she will be raising difficult issues and to invite the client to do the same.

The Contracting Discussion

The basic model for a contracting discussion is as follows:

Step 1: The consultant starts with his or her definition of the consulting project: "My understanding of the effort is..."

Step 2: The consultant asks the client to state his or her expectations: "What do you expect from the project and from me?"

Step 3: The consultant states his or her capabilities and requirements of the client: "What I believe I can do effectively is... What I feel I need from you for this to be successful is ..."

Step 4: The consultant raises his or her own concerns, and the possible risks, and surfaces those of the client: "My biggest concern is..." What's your biggest concern? What constraints do you see in this?"

Step 5: The consultant summarizes the expectations, requirements, and concerns of both sides and gets confirmation. "To recap, your expectations are..."

Consultant Straight-talk Versus Double-talk

Before looking at some examples of contracting, let's distinguish between consultant straight-talk and consultant double-talk. Just as there is great pressure to proceed without a contract, there is often great pressure to play false roles, speak in vague euphemisms, or paper over concerns — consultant double-talk. For contracting (and consulting in general) to be effective, the consultant must use straight-talk. Straight-talk means that the consultant puts into words, carefully but directly, what he or she is thinking or feeling. Here are some examples of common consulting situations, the double-talk that a consultant would be tempted to use, and the straight-talk that would be much more effective.

Situation #1: Diagnosing Client Needs

Client Statement: "My team needs teambuilding."

Consultant Thoughts and Feelings: I'm not sure that's what the client really needs. I'm feeling pushed into an intervention.

Consultant Double-talk: "I'd like to talk to the team to get their views on the team before we begin."

Consultant Straight-talk: "I'd like to diagnose the team myself. If teambuilding is not what's needed, it will waste your time and make the team more cynical."

Situation #2: Presenting A Progress Update

Client Statement: "I'd like you to present our progress to the Steering Team."

Consultant Thoughts and Feelings: I would be presenting the material secondhand. I feel I'm being used as a trial balloon or shield.

Consultant Double-talk: "I'm not sure I could cover all of the issues or answer their questions."

Consultant Straight-talk: "I would only feel comfortable presenting the progress that I know about firsthand."

Situation #3: Predicting Success

Client Question: "It's important that this training works. Will they like it?"

Consultant Thoughts and Feelings: I hope so! Some of the topics and theories might make them uncomfortable. I'm getting the message that they want to hear positive answers.

Consultant Double-talk: "No problem — they'll love it."

Consultant Straight-talk: "The training is designed to be interesting and has been well-received by other groups. I don't know beforehand how they'll react to some of the content."

Situation #4: Discussing Time Commitments

Client Statement: "I don't have a lot of time for this."

Consultant Thoughts and Feelings: I'm getting the message that I better not impose and wear out my welcome. I feel resistance from the client.

Consultant Double-talk: "I understand. We will be efficient and move quickly."

Consultant Straight-talk: "This does take time. I'm afraid there's no way around that. You seem unsure of the benefits of this process."

Situation #5: Describing The Need For Follow-up

Client Statement: "You're spending a lot of time on follow-up. Is that what makes this work?"

Consultant Thoughts and Feelings: I'm getting the message that I better defend my use of time on follow-up. I feel that the client isn't aware of the importance of his involvement.

Consultant Double-talk: "Yes, training by itself often doesn't produce action. Follow-up is the key ingredient."

Consultant Straight-talk: "Follow-up together with your visible support are two of the critical elements. Are you concerned about the time I'm spending on follow-up?

Situation #6: The Confusing Statement

Client Statement: "I feel that this is one of the tools in our toolbox along with a number of our other projects, and that if we can make significant progress on this in the context of those other projects, that would be good."

Consultant Thoughts and Feelings: I have no idea what he's talking about, but it sounds like how executives talk. I'm getting the message that I should agree, but I feel uncomfortable about the vagueness of the discussion.

Consultant Double-talk: "Yes, it's certainly a key tool and progress would be good."

Consultant Straight-talk: "I'm sorry, I'm not following you."

Situation #7: Can We Take A Shortcut?

Client Statement: "I don't have time to get off the bicycle in order to fix it. We have to do this on the run. This initial training can only take a half-day."

Consultant Thoughts and Feelings: I'm getting the message that I better take the time I can get. I feel the pressure to minimize the impact and magnitude of my intervention.

Consultant Double-talk: "O.K., we'll do the best we can."

Consultant Straight-talk: "The initial training requires at least two days. Shortcutting it would not do justice to the process. How do you feel about that?"

Situation #8: Observing The Leader's Meetings

Client Statement: "I don't think you need to attend our meetings. We cover a variety of topics in those meetings that are beyond the scope of the project."

Consultant Thoughts and Feelings: I'm getting the message that I'm not invited to these meetings and that the leader does not want a coach observing his team leadership skills and giving him feedback. I feel I'm being excluded from key situations.

Consultant Double-talk: "I understand. I'd like to observe your meetings in action at some point, though."

Consultant Straight-talk: "I feel that, as a team leader, you should have the same coaching as the other team leaders, and that we should analyze your meeting in terms of the criteria for an effective team meeting. I realize it's unusual for a non-team member to attend, but I believe this is essential. How do you feel about that?"

Situation #9: Being Honest About Expertise

Client Question: "Are you going to be able to help the teams figure out their performance measures?"

Client Thoughts and Feelings: I better appear capable and willing. I'm getting the message that I should give a positive, uncomplicated answer.

Consultant Double-talk: "Yes, I can help them do that."

Consultant Straight-talk: "I know the theory of team performance measures, but I am not familiar with your department's work. I will need to work with whoever in your department knows the most about reporting and controls."

Situation #10: Discussing Disadvantages

Client Statement: "I'm concerned about the time and paperwork involved in the documentation of team meeting agendas and team action records. I want to avoid that."

Consultant Thoughts and Feelings: I'm getting the message to agree to avoid paperwork. I feel concerned because part of what makes a team system work is the discipline of structured meetings and documented action steps.

Consultant Double-talk: "No problem. We'll make sure to keep the paperwork to a minimum."

Consultant Straight-talk: "I share your desire to avoid bureaucracy. However, I do feel that team meeting agendas and team action records are an essential part of team management. Are you saying you're concerned about those tools?"

Situation #11: Getting A Rush Order

Client Statement: "I'd like to do a modified version of the class and a good time for my team would be two weeks from now."

Consultant Thoughts and Feelings: I'm being rushed into doing a customized class. I'm getting the message that I should agree.

Consultant Double-talk: "I'll do the best I can. My schedule is pretty tight."

Consultant Straight-talk: "Two weeks is too soon for a major modified version, given my other commitments. I can do the regular version in two weeks. I believe I could do a modified version in six weeks. Which would be better for you?"

Situation #12: Involving A New Function

Client Statement: "I'd like to get the sales and marketing groups involved in the change effort. But they can't get the same training that operations got. They're different. Can you develop something else?"

Consultant Thoughts and Feelings: I'm being asked to change the principles and concepts to be more palatable to a certain group. This feels like we're watering down our effort.

Consultant Double-talk: "I'm sure we can modify the content to fit their needs."

Consultant Straight-talk: "I think it's important that the content remains consistent throughout the organization, and that we don't pull the teeth out of it as we go along. However, I'm sure that operations can provide examples of how the content applies to sales and marketing, and how they affect each other's work. I can build those examples into the training. Do you agree that it's important that the training remain consistent?"

Example Of A Contracting Discussion

The following is an example of a contracting discussion between an internal consultant and her top client, a department head, at the start of an implementation of team management. The consultant has previously presented an implementation plan to the department head, who approved the plan. Now the consultant would like to ensure that she and the department head have the same expectations for the implementation.

Consultant: "Thanks for seeing me."

Client: "Sure."

Consultant: "How is everything going?"

Client: "Things are going pretty well. I'm looking forward to starting team management. You said you'd like to talk about our expectations for the implementation?"

Consultant: "Yes. I know we have a plan that covers the goals and specific steps of the implementation. Still, I'd like to make sure I understand your requirements for the effort and I also have some requests for you. I want to make sure that we don't have any communication gaps and that we're expecting the same things."

Client: "O.K. Go ahead."

Results   *Consultant:* "Let me start with results. Our plan says that our main goal is timeliness—that all projects in the department will be hitting all their milestones within twelve months. I want to confirm that that is your measure of success for the team management implementation."

Client: "Yes, it is."

Consultant: "What other results are you looking for?"

Client: "Well, I'm not sure we put it explicitly in the plan, but I want quality and cost to stay constant as we improve timeliness."

Consultant: "How would you measure quality?"

Client: "By customer feedback. Customers should report no decrease in the quality of our service as we work on timeliness."

Consultant: "So if our projects are hitting all milestones twelve months from now and customer surveys show no decrease in ratings compared to the past year, you would consider the implementation a success."

Client: "Yes."

Consultant: "What about costs? You mentioned that they should stay constant also."

Client: "Yes. We should be able to hit our milestones without increasing costs."

Consultant: "How should we measure costs?"

Client: "The primary driver of costs in this department is number of personnel. I guess what I'm really saying is that we should be able to hit our milestones without increasing the number of personnel."

Consultant: "So success twelve months from now looks like all projects in the department on-time against milestones without customer survey scores showing a decrease and without increasing the number of personnel.

Client: "Yes, that's right."

Roadmap

Consultant: "As you know from the implementation plan, our basic roadmap is that we will do orientations for all teams, followed by four days of training for all team leaders and members, with weekly consulting follow-up for all teams. What are your thoughts on this?"

Client: "How will you handle teams that need more follow-up than that?"

Consultant: "There are three choices: Those teams don't get more follow-up and just progress more slowly; I can shift my follow-up time from teams that are progressing well; or I can call in additional help such as an outside consultant. We should know in the first two months whether weekly follow-up will be enough for all the teams."

Client: "O.K., let's decide on that in month two."

Consultant: "What other thoughts do you have about our basic roadmap?"

Client: "None. I think it's covered well in the implementation plan. I feel comfortable with it."

Roles

Consultant: "In terms of roles, I see myself as communications coordinator, trainer, consultant, advisor to you, and consultant to your team. Does that sound right to you?"

Client: "Yes, that's how I see you."

Consultant: "What problems do you foresee in my playing any of these roles?"

Client: "None in particular."

Consultant: "Well, if a problem were to develop, in which of my roles do you think it would probably occur?"

Client: "Probably consulting to my team."

Consultant: "How so?"

Client: "Well, you'll be an unknown quantity to them. We've never had anyone sit in with us for the purpose of observing and giving us feedback."

Consultant: "What do you see as the best way to handle that?"

Client: "I can say something to them about your role and its benefits to the team at our next meeting. I'll remind them that all the other teams are going through the same thing and ask for their cooperation."

Consultant: "That's sounds good. Any other possible role problems that you see for me?"

Client: "No. Just my team getting comfortable with you as its consultant."

Consultant: "Let me ask you this. How do you see your role in the implementation?"

Client: "I see myself as providing leadership for the implementation."

Consultant: "I certainly support that. What are your thoughts on the specifics of that?"

Client: "Communicating about the effort and setting a good example."

Consultant: "I agree. I would suggest that the specifics of leading the effort fall into three categories: modeling, communication, and participation. By modeling, I mean that people should see you demonstrating the team management skills. In terms of communication, people should hear you talking about team management in your formal and informal talks. In terms of participation, people should see you in the training, having team meetings, and so forth. I see part of my consulting role as helping you do those things. How does that sound?"

Client: "That sounds good. I will take the lead in those areas. But I'd also like you to prompt me in those areas."

Consultant: "I'll be glad to do that. You're willing to play those roles?"

Client: "Yes, certainly."

Responsibilities   *Consultant:* "Let me say a little more about the responsibilities in my roles. In my communications role, I would like to interview you and your team about team management and, based on your comments, develop a presentation on team management that you and your direct reports can use in orientation sessions. In my training role, I will conduct the training and be responsible for training materials and logistics. Later, in my follow-up role, I will meet with each team leader individually each week and attend each team meeting every two weeks. Are those your expectations?"

Client: "Yes, I agree. In addition to consulting with me and with my team, that's what I expect you to do."

Consultant: "What about the responsibility to hold people in the department accountable for progress."

Client: "I see that as my responsibility and my team's. If you'll track progress, I will make sure that people understand the importance of making progress and I will pay appropriate attention to those who do."

Resources   *Consultant:* "In terms of resources, my understanding is that I'm on this 100% of my time, with all expenses coming out of my budget. I also assume that I can call on people in finance, engineering, and marketing if we need help with measures, processes, or customers."

Client: "Yes, that's correct."

Reporting   *Consultant:* "How would you like me to report progress to you?"

Client: "I would like a monthly written progress report. We can meet each month to go over that."

Consultant: "Fine. However, I would also like to talk to you more frequently about progress. Could we meet every two weeks?"

Client: "Why is that necessary? I'll see the progress in the report."

Consultant: "I would like to get guidance from you on what I'm doing more often than monthly. And frankly, I would like to be able to ask for your help more often than once per month."

Client: "How about if you voice-mail me whenever you want about what's happening and we meet face-to-face if we need to, based on we discuss in the voice mails."

Relationship   *Consultant:* "O.K., let's try that. That's gets into my final topic — some specifics about how we will work together."

Client: "I don't understand. Didn't we just cover that?"

Consultant: "I want to make sure that I'm clear in my mind about two things: how we will make decisions, and what to do if one of us feels something's going wrong.

Client: "I expect you to make all decisions related to your roles. If a decision would greatly change the results we expect or the roadmap, I want to be in on it. If you feel something's going wrong, let me know. I will do the same."

Consultant: "That sounds good. In that vein, I want to say that I feel it's my responsibility to raise difficult issues and I hope you will do the same. I may offer suggestions or feedback that makes us both uncomfortable, but I see that as part of my job. Do I have your permission to do that?

Client: "Yes, you do. I want you to do that."

Consultant: "O.K., that's everything. Thanks. I'd like to type up my notes on this and give you a copy so that we have a record."

Sample Contracting Document With The Leader

The following is a sample memorandum of understanding that would follow the contracting discussion above.

MEMORANDUM

TO: Bill Anderson, Department Head

FROM: Diane Lambert, Internal Consultant

SUB: Memo of Understanding on Team Management

This is my understanding of our combined expectations for the implementation of Team Management:

Results. Our objective is to have all projects in the department on-time against milestones without customer survey scores showing a decrease and without increasing the number of personnel. We will implement a team management system as a means of accomplishing that objective. Teams will be formed and the teams will define and track team performance measures. The teams will examine the processes by which they do their work and meet regularly to review progress, share information, plan, and problem-solve. Teams will have action plans that impact timeliness of deliverables. In the first six months, we expect to see "soft" results, such as teams having effective meetings, using charts, and communicating better with other teams. By the end of twelve months, we expect to see "hard" results in terms of timeliness of deliverables against milestones on all projects.

Roadmap. The main interventions will be orientation sessions, training, and consulting follow-up. Every member of the department will attend an orientation session conducted by the consultant and a member of the senior team. All team leaders and team members will receive four days of training.

After the training, every team leader, including yourself, will be coached once per week for twelve months. The consultant will attend the team meeting of each team (including the senior team's) every other week.

Roles. I see myself as the communications coordinator, trainer, consultant, advisor to you, and consultant to your team. I will also be the consultant to the teams in your department.

I understand that your role will be leader of the senior team, role model, participant, chief communicator about the process, and manager of the effort.

Responsibilities. In my communications role, I will develop a presentation on team management, based on interviews with you and your team, that you and your team members can use in orientation sessions. In my training role, I will conduct the training and be responsible for training materials and logistics. In my coaching role, I will meet with each team leader individually each week and attend each team meeting every two weeks. I will help the team leaders prepare, observe team meetings, provide feedback to the team and to the team leader, and follow-up on team action plans. In my advisor role, I will report progress directly to you in writing and by voice mail, and we will discuss issues and needed action.

I understand that in your role as model, you will operate the team in team-management style and demonstrate team-management skills. In your role as participant, you will attend the training, receive coaching, and implement an action plan. In your role as communicator, you will communicate frequently in person and in writing about team management. In your role as manager, you will use the senior team as a forum for making decisions about the direction of the implementation and for establishing accountability for progress.

Resources. I understand that I am in this assignment 100% of my time. All expenses related to training and outside consulting come out of my budget. I may call on expertise in finance, engineering, and marketing for help as needed. As noted in the implementation plan, team leaders can be expected to spend at least three hours minimum per week on team management. The team members will spend approximately an hour each week in team meetings.

Reporting. On the last day of every month, I will write a monthly status report stating activities that were planned to be accomplished, activities that were actually accomplished, positive results if any and success stories, actions that I will take and actions that I ask you to take. We will meet face-to-face on a monthly basis to review the status report. I will voice-mail you as needed and we will meet more often as needed.

Relationship. During our monthly meeting we will do a level-check by asking each other, "Is there anything that I should be doing that I'm not? Is there any advice or coaching you have for me? Is there anything worrying you now about the change effort?" I feel that it is my role to raise difficult issues and I request that you do so as well. I will keep all matters confidential. I may have to present some information to you anonymously to maintain the confidence and privacy of the participants.

If there is anything here that is different than your understanding, please let me know and we can discuss it more fully. Thank you for your candor and I look forward to a successful effort.

Sample "Standard" Contract With Team Leaders

The following is an example of a "standard" contract to clarify expectations between the consultant and each of the team leaders participating in the implementation.

MEMORANDUM

TO: Team Leaders

FROM: Diane Lambert, Internal Consultant

SUB: Memo of Understanding on Team Management

This is to clarify our expectations as we begin the implementation of Team Management.

Results. The objective of Team Management is to have all projects in the department on-time against milestones without customer survey scores showing a decrease and without increasing the number of personnel. Teams will develop action plans that impact timeliness of deliverables in their projects. The teams will examine the processes by which they do their work and meet regularly to review progress, share information, plan, and problem-solve.

In the first six months, we expect that the teams will accomplish the major implementation milestones: identify processes, identify customers, identify team measures, analyze processes, begin team meetings, and develop action plans. These milestones will be explained further in the Team Management training.

In the first six months, we also expect that the teams will begin practicing team-management skills, such as having effective meetings, using charts, and communicating better with other teams. By the end of twelve months, we expect to see results in terms of timeliness of deliverables against milestones on all projects.

Roadmap. The main interventions will be orientation sessions, training, and consulting follow-up. Every member of the department will attend an orientation session conducted by the consultant and a member of the senior team. All team leaders and team members will receive four days of training. After the training, every team leader will be coached once per week for twelve months. The consultant will attend the team meeting of each team (including the senior team's) every other week.

Roles. I will conduct the Team Management training and serve as consultant to you and your team.

Your role as a team leader in Team Management is to be a participant, role model, and leader of the team.

Responsibilities. In my training role, I will conduct the training and be responsible for training materials and logistics. In my coaching role, I will meet with each team leader individually each week and attend each team meeting every two weeks. I will help each team leader prepare for team meetings, observe the team meetings, provide feedback to the team and to the team leader, and follow-up and advise on team action plans.

In the role of participant, you are expected to attend the training, receive coaching, and accomplish the implementation milestones. In the role of model, you are expected to demonstrate the team-management skills covered in the training. In the role of leader, you are expected to conduct regular team meetings and implement a team action plan.

Resources. Our implementation of Team Management requires each team leader spend at least three hours minimum per week on team management, roughly an hour one-to-one with the consultant, an hour preparing for the team meeting, and an hour in the team meeting. The team members will spend approximately an hour each week in the team meetings.

I am a resource to your team on any issue related to customer focus, team functioning, organizational communication, process operation, and any issue that affects quality, cost, and speed. You can contact me at any time.

Reporting. On the last day of every month, I will write a monthly status report to the senior team stating activities that were planned to be accomplished, activities that were actually accomplished, positive results if any and success stories, actions that I will take and actions that the senior team is requested to take. In this regard, I will be asking you about your progress regularly.

Relationship. At every contact, we will do a level-check by asking, "Is there any advice or coaching you have for me? Is there anything worrying you now about the change effort?" I will keep all private discussions confidential. However, your team's progress in the implementation is "public record," and will be part of my normal reporting. I feel that it is my role to raise difficult issues and I request that you do so as well.

If there is anything here that is different than your understanding, please let me know and we can discuss it. I look forward to a successful effort.

A Final Note On Contracting

The contracting discussion and document is the *starting point* in establishing an effective consultant-client relationship. Trust means matching our actions to our words. Being trusted means being predictable — the other person knows how we are going to act. The clearest, most genuine contract will be invalidated if the consultant does not behave according to it.

Summary

In this chapter, we described the importance of contracting and its key elements, distinguished between consultant straight-talk and double-talk, and offered some examples of contracts. In the next chapter, we will explore consulting deliverables.

7

Consulting Deliverables

7

Communication As A Deliverable

Training As A Deliverable

Consulting As A Deliverable

Designing New Systems As A Deliverable

Consulting Deliverables

The fourth step in the consulting cycle is Deliver. In this step the consultant provides the interventions that have been planned and contracted. These interventions should help the participants make progress in the change effort.

The objectives of this chapter are to describe the basics of providing service in the area of communication, training, coaching, and designing systems.

The model for change suggests four basic services in helping people change. Awareness is achieved through communication. The change agent must be a publicist, and help the leader be a visionary. Understanding is achieved through training. The change agent must be a trainer, and must encourage the leader to be both a teacher and learner. Implementation requires coaching and management. The change agent must help, coach, and support, and must encourage the leader to make personal changes and manage others to do the same. The Change stage requires that new systems be installed. The change agent must be a designer of the new systems, encouraging the leader to build them.

Communication As A Deliverable

Some key elements of a successful communication effort are the following.

Write A Manifesto

A manifesto is a public declaration of principles or intentions. The consultant should create a manifesto about the change initiative, that is, a concise, easy-to-read document that introduces the effort. The document should:

- Explain what the change effort is and what it isn't.

- Describe the approach that is being used, such as total quality management or process reengineering.

- Explain how the change effort is linked to the business strategy of the organization.

- Describe how the change effort is linked to other initiatives occurring in the organization.

- Describe the case for action, that is, why the change is needed, its expected benefits, and what might happen to the organization if it fails to change.

- Relate the change to the vision, mission, and principles of the organization.

- Establish consistent terminology and clarify any expected misunderstandings about vocabulary, such as the terms "customer," "team," or "process."

- Establish clear expectations as to what will happen, when it will happen, and how associates will be involved.

- Refer to any relevant customer or employee survey data.

- Describe the roles of the leaders and change agents as well as the change services available, such as training and consulting.

- Describe the history of the change effort and any preparatory steps taken thus far.

The senior team should contribute to, edit, and "bless" it as a document of the change effort. The manifesto should be widely distributed; video and electronic versions should be created as appropriate.

The Case For Action

The most important aspect of the manifesto is probably the case for action. If the associates of the organization develop a basic awareness of the need to change, many other questions can be answered as they arise. The manifesto should focus on what positive outcomes for the organization are expected if the change occurs successfully. Is the change a necessary component of growth, profitability, and security? What will happen if the change does not occur successfully? How will competitiveness be affected? How will the status quo fare in the future? What will customers be expecting in the future that the organization is not now capable of delivering? What future edge will competitors have in the future unless the organization changes?

A worthwhile exercise is to ask managers to write two stories. The first story is a "success story" five years in the future. Imagine that *The Wall Street Journal* or *Fortune* is writing an article five years from now about your organization's successful change and its impact on the business. What would be covered in the article? What would have been accomplished? What types of change would have occurred in the strategy, operation, and culture of the organization? What obstacles would have been overcome?

Now, have the managers write the second story. It is a "failure story." Imagine that the business journalists are writing a story five years hence about how the organization failed to change and thus ran into business difficulties. What would be covered in that article? Why weren't the organization's efforts to change successful? What went wrong? What obstacles were not overcome? To what outside forces did the organization become vulnerable?

Initial Communication

Communicate about the change through all of the regular communication channels in the organization. Keep in mind the "7 x 7 rule" — communicate seven times using seven different media. Provide slide presentations for all senior managers so that they can make presentations about the change.

Ongoing Communication

Communicate progress about both activities and results in the change. Use company-wide publications, new hire orientations, training classes, departmental meetings, awareness seminars, team meetings, procedure manuals, associate handbooks, videos, brochures, bulletin boards, posters, and signs to communicate the message. These communication media should also provide positive recognition for all progress.

Training As A Deliverable

Here are the basics on conducting and designing training.

Guidelines For Conducting Training

1. Start with the objective. Whenever you design, prepare, or present training, make sure you have clearly identified in your own mind what the learners should be able to do when the training is completed.

2. Outline the material. Give the most time to the most important learning objectives. Logically connect each section of the outline to the sections preceding and following it. In other words, make sure that the material "flows." The logical connections are the "transitions" between the topics in your presentation.

3. Describe the benefits. When you introduce a new topic, the audience is secretly thinking: "So what? Why is this worth my attention?" Explain why the topic is important and worth learning. If people are resistant or disinterested, the benefits of the topic have not been clearly presented.

4. Use a flipchart or overhead projector. Visual aids help the learners follow the presentation.

5. Use "real English." Imagine that you are presenting the topic of assertiveness. The dictionary defines assertiveness as "to defend or maintain one's rights, to express oneself forcefully or boldly." In real English, assertiveness is "getting what you want without trampling over the other guy." Real English works better in training.

6. Use examples. People learn much better from examples than from definitions and descriptions. For example, after defining a feedback system, use a speedometer as an example of a feedback system which lets a driver know how fast he or she is going. Examples are particularly important when people are confused. You should have at least one good example for each key point.

7. Prepare for questions. Ask yourself: "What will they ask on this topic? What would I ask?" Have answers to these questions.

8. Get the participants to talk. Ask the participants their opinions. Use open-ended questions. Call people by name and ask direct questions. Start by asking easy questions and work up to the tough ones. Raise interesting or controversial issues. Reinforce participation when you get it.

9. Have people practice new skills. People learn by doing. Get the participants talking and doing things in the training.

10. Include summaries and reviews. People can only remember seven plus-or-minus two chunks of information at one time. Help the learners organize and remember information by summarizing each topic and frequently reviewing.

11. Listen. People learn best when they are taken seriously. Listening is how you show someone that you take them seriously. Also, people tend to agree with you once you have agreed with them. Listen and look for the merit in people's ideas before expecting them to accept your ideas. Rephrasing defuses emotion. People sometimes become defensive, argumentative, or anxious when faced with newness. Your first response to these emotions should be rephrasing. Say, "What I hear you saying is..." and give your understanding of the person's view. That person will eventually be willing to listen to your view.

12. Give clear instructions. Write the instructions on the flipchart or overhead. Give an example of how to do the exercise. Repeat instructions several times.

13. Do the exercises yourself. The best way to identify the correct answers and to help the learners is to do the exercises yourself, in advance. Consider this basic preparation.

14. People need both positive and corrective feedback. Positive feedback is easy enough, but giving corrective feedback can be uncomfortable. Here are some phrases that may help you: "I'm going to disagree with you and let me tell you why..." "That's not quite it. How about...?" "I think a better answer is..." "The way I would answer that is..."

15. Learning should be fun. Take a relaxed and playful approach to training. Look for interesting examples and demonstrations.

16. People can only listen intently to about 20 minutes of lecture. Keep your lectures short. Even professional public speakers only speak for one to two hours; 20 minutes is plenty for classroom lectures. Use exercises, discussions, and breaks to keep your listeners alert.

E.S.T.R.A.

A good way to remember the basic principles of training is E.S.T.R.A.:

E = Explain. Explain what your topic is, what your objectives are, and why the topic is important.

S = Show. If you are teaching a concept, give examples. If you are teaching a skill, demonstrate it. Use outlines and diagrams to provide clear mental pictures.

T = Talk them through it. Have the participants try the new skill or knowledge in a learning activity. Talk them through it with them doing at least 50% of it. Prompt, remind, and point out details.

R = Reinforce. Reinforce what they do well. Tell them when they do it right. In the beginning, acknowledge small improvements.

A = Advise. Give advice or tips for how to do it better next time. Set your learners up for success when they use the new skill in the "real world."

Designing A Training Course

To design a training course, address these ten topics: 1) objectives, 2) slant, 3) content, 4) methods, 5) structure, 6) preparation, 7) materials, 8) enjoyment, 9) timing, and 10) logistics.

1. Objectives. What skills are the participants supposed to learn? What knowledge are the participants supposed to gain? What feelings are the participants supposed to experience? What experiential learnings or discoveries (*ah-ha's*) are the participants supposed to have? What actions are the participants supposed to take as a result of the class?

2. Slant. Is there a special "slant" to the audience or situation? Slant is a unique angle on the content, design, or presentation based on characteristics of the participants or situation. The slant may affect your choice of teaching methods, learning materials, and timing. Examples of "slants" are:

- The participants are not used to sitting.
- The participants have had a great deal of training before.
- The training is being forced on the participants.
- The participants are used to presentations with humor.
- The participants are from different locations.
- The participants have many opinions about the content and like to talk.

3. Content. What is the content (definitions, facts, and concepts) of each block of the course? What is the necessary background material? What theories and models are relevant? Read all related books and articles. You will not use everything, but the background will help you answer questions correctly and confidently. Keep in mind that until people learn something new in the class, they do not consider it worthwhile.

4. Methods. Given the objectives, slant, and content of each block of the course, what are the best teaching methods? Options are:

_____ Lecture

_____ Large-group discussions

_____ Small-group discussions

_____ Case method

_____ Paper-and-pencil, answer-the-question exercises

_____ Games and simulations

_____ Role plays and behavior rehearsals

_____ Demonstrations

_____ Behavior modeling

_____ Videotape rehearsal

_____ Socratic method

_____ Field trips

_____ Research-and-present

_____ Show-and-tell

_____ Programmed instruction (fill-in the answer and check-it)

_____ Individualized instruction (study guides, mastery-based quizzes)

_____ "Talk through it, walk through it, do it."

_____ "See one, do one, teach one."

_____ Model-building and movie-making

_____ In-box exercises

_____ Debates

_____ Find-the-bug

_____ Multimedia instruction

_____ Other: _____

5. Structure. Outline each block of the course by identifying: a) learning objectives, b) teaching method, c) introduction or transition, d) benefits of the topic, e) teaching materials, f) key points, g) learning activities, that is, ways of learning, h) exercises, that is, ways of demonstrating learning, i) summary points, and j) transition to the next section or course wrap-up.

6. Preparation. Prepare notes and visual material:

_____ Lectures

_____ Examples

_____ Stories

_____ Benefits

_____ Transitions

_____ Facilitation questions

_____ Instructions to learning activities and exercises

_____ Preparation of overheads or pre-written flipcharts

7. Materials. Prepare materials that the participants will use during and after the class.

8. Enjoyment. Is the training designed to be enjoyable? Some topics are more intrinsically interesting than others where the delivery has to provide the enjoyment. In most cases, the presentation, structure, pace, stories, and discussion make the training interesting, rather than the content itself.

Even modest people find it fun to talk about themselves and their own situations. Novel approaches make things interesting. Don't use the same teaching approach for all of your content. Enjoy the class yourself.

9. Timing. Check the timing, logical order, and emotional balance of each block of content and of the class as a whole. Logical order means that the overall class and each content block should have an opening, a body, and a close, or transition. Logical order also means first things first. For example, you should explain the importance of team meetings before explaining team meeting agendas. Emotional balance means that the beginning should be upbeat, the hard work should be in the middle, and the ending should also be upbeat.

Points to remember are:

- Lectures should be short.
- Participants relax when they get to talk.
- Do something active right after lunch.
- The longer the activity, the bigger the learning point should be.
- Avoid repeated "technique-ing." For example, generating lists of problems, ideas, or benefits is a useful technique but it should not be overdone.

10. Logistics. Check:

_____ Room temperature

_____ Physical layout

_____ Warm-up exercises each morning and afternoon

_____ Housekeeping issues such as coffee, breaks, phones, restrooms

_____ Pre-work. Don't count on completion before the class.

_____ Homework. If you give homework, follow up on it.

_____ Announcements of the training

_____ Participant lists

_____ Participant Evaluation. A universal evaluation is:

   1. What did you like?

   2. What would you change?

   3. What did you find most useful?

   4. What did you find least useful?

   5. Comments on instructor's teaching style.

Consulting As A Deliverable

Consulting as a deliverable can be divided into consulting one-to-one and consulting to a team. Before addressing each, let's look at the emotional differences between consulting and training. Since many consultants are, or were trainers, it is important to note how the two deliverables "feel."

Consulting Is Different From Training

Consulting is emotionally different from training. For the trainer, the workshop is a fairly controllable place. The trainer determines the content, timing, and to a large degree, the emotional tone of the class. The trainer must know people and what they find interesting, and must be able to "read the room." To succeed, the trainer relies heavily on himself or herself, focusing on preparation and rehearsal. By definition, the trainer usually knows the answers to participant questions. Every class has discrete content. The trainer is reaction-oriented, sensitive to and reinforced by how the participants respond. It is important to the trainer that the participants like the class. The trainer is always mentally one step ahead of the participants because the trainer knows what's going to happen next. Finally, the trainer wins most of the time. Trainers live in fear of a class "bombing." If a training class "doesn't work," the trainer modifies it quickly.

For the consultant, the workplace is much less controllable than the workshop. The participants don't graduate, and questions, problems, and emotional reactions occur at any time. In addition to knowing people, the consultant must know the business and how a given set of theories and prin-ciples applies to it. The consultant can do very little alone and must rely heavily on the client. Rather than knowing the answers in advance, the consultant must find answers. The consultant must be result-oriented. Hard results are more important than subjective reactions, and in the midst of change, positive reactions become increasingly rare. Rather than knowing what's going to happen next, the consultant usually feels one step behind, or at best, side-by-side with the client. Finally, the consultant wins some and loses some. The workplace is too complex to produce a steady string of victories for the consultant.

Consulting One-To-One: The SOLAR Model

A consulting contact can be as structured and focused as a training class or sales call. Several things should happen in any consulting contact. For an effective consulting contact, remember "SOLAR" (see Figure 7.1):

- <u>S</u>ocialize — Begin the session with informal conversation

- <u>O</u>bjective — Establish the objective of the contact

- <u>L</u>isten — Use listening skills to assess the client's situation

- <u>A</u>dvise — Influence the client by making recommendations, coaching, persuading, confronting, or helping to solve a problem

- <u>R</u>ecord — Identify and record specific next steps

<u>S</u>ocialize

The aim of socializing is to relate to the client on a personal level. Socializing in consulting contact is equivalent to an "icebreaker" exercise in a training

Figure 7.1 The SOLAR Model for a Consulting Contact

class. The object is to establish a pleasant working atmosphere and to get a reading on the client's orientation to the change effort. The consultant asks such questions as:

- "How are you doing?"
- "How is work going?"
- "How was your weekend?"

The consultant must be sensitive to the client's interest in socializing and the amount of chatting that is socially acceptable in the local culture. The consultant must also be aware of how personal to be: "How was your weekend"... might be too personal in some cases. Depending on the circumstances,

233

one might spend 30 seconds or ten minutes socializing.

One goal of socializing is to check how busy the client is. Although the consultant should not let busy days become a way to avoid a contact, occasionally an emergency or unseen circumstance may be a valid reason to postpone a meeting.

Another goal of the consultant is to be a reinforcing person. The client should be glad to see the consultant. The consultant should be socially skilled, aware of the client's interests, and upbeat about life and the change effort. The consultant also seeks to establish commonality. In what ways are the consultant and client similar? Do they have similar values related to work, goals, success, family, and relaxation? The more commonality between client and consultant, the more likely the client will be to give credence to the consultant's recommendations. A way to establish commonality is to socialize a bit during the contacts.

Finally, the consultant would like to get a reading on the client's current reaction to the change effort. Is the client energized or weary, hopeful or cynical, pleased or disappointed with the changes thus far? Again, the brief "warm-up" conversation is a way to gauge that.

Objective

The purpose of stating the objective of the consulting contact is to identify plainly the consultant's goal for the session and to confirm that it is also the client's goal. Stating the consulting objective establishes a clear expectation for productive dialogue. Examples of stating the objective are:

- "Our agreement from last time was that we would go over the agenda for your upcoming team meeting."
- "What I'd like us to accomplish today is to determine whether the control limits for the team's control charts need to be recalculated."
- "My objective for this meeting is to get your reaction to the last team meeting and to share my feedback on that meeting."

It is important to end with, "How does that sound to you?" The consultant should have a clear objective for the session, but it is just as important that the client agrees that it is a worthwhile objective.

Listen

Listening refers to using reflective skills to assess the client's current situation and to determine how best to help. The consultant can start the discussion with:

- "How do you feel it's going?"
- "What are your thoughts on the process?"

Prompting, rephrasing, open-ended questions, body language, and empathy are all critical to the consultant's sense of the client's current status (see Chapter 3). The consultant listens for the client's situation. Which best describes the client's current circumstance?

- No Problem.
- No Understanding.
- No Buy-in.

- No Action.
- No Success.

No Problem means that the client is cooperating, has not encountered any difficulties, and simply needs to take a new step. No Problem requires *recommending* by the consultant. *No Understanding* means that the client is confused about a concept or has not mastered a skill. No Understanding requires *coaching* by the consultant. *No Buy-in* means that the client is unconvinced of the value of a concept, principle, or action step. No Buy-in requires *persuading* by the Consultant. *No Action* means that the client has not completed action steps and has not put the skills and concepts into practice. No Action requires *confronting* by the consultant. *No Success* means that the

Figure 7.2 Listening and the Five Skills of Advising

client has taken action but has encountered difficulties. No Success requires *solving* by the consultant (see Figure 7.2).

Advise

Advising is the consultant's opportunity to influence the client. Advising means applying the consultant's observation, experience, or expertise to the situation. The consultant recommends, coaches, persuades, confronts, or solves

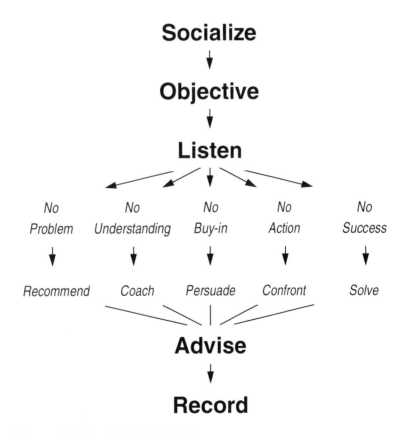

Figure 7.3 The SOLAR Model

a problem to accomplish the objective of the contact. The five skills of Advising (see Chapter 3) come into play in the Advising step of the SOLAR Model (see Figure 7.3).

Recommending

Recommending is the consulting response if there is No Problem. The client has made progress up to this point and is basically asking, "What do I do next?" or "What do you think I ought to do now?" The consultant should offer advice or suggest a next step. Examples of Recommending statements are:

- "The next step in the process is..."
- "How comfortable are you with the next step, which is...?"
- "What can I do to help you with the next step?"

Coaching

Coaching is the consulting response if there is No Understanding. The client may say, "I don't get it" or "I think I'm doing something wrong." Or the consultant may sense a lack of skill or understanding. The consultant must teach the concept or help the client develop the skill. Examples of Coaching statements are:

- "One of the concepts from the training that applies here is..."
- "A concept that might add value in this situation is..."
- "Fully implementing the approach would mean that you would be..."
- "A way that I would see this working is..."
- "Let's draw a distinction between 'teams' and 'working groups.'"
- "Some of the other teams are applying this concept like this..."
- "The next step your team needs to work on is to use the seven basic tools

of quality to analyze that problem."

- "It is important to make progress on cross-training."
- "You don't have team ground-rules completed at this point."
- "When do you think you can do that by?"
- "Let's meet again next Thursday to go over the progress on completing the customer survey."

Persuading

Persuading is the consulting response if there is No Buy-in. If the consultant senses that the client is not "sold" on the objective, principle, or theory, then the consultant must present the idea in a convincing manner. Again, the client might announce, "I don't buy this," or might signal uncertainty with questions, body language, or debate. An example of a Persuading statement is:

- "What about trying a teambuilding session? In a teambuilding session, the team members would raise what they see as the strengths and areas for improvement of the team and the team could talk them through. Everyone would have a chance to have a say and clear the air. The benefits will be that some issues might surface that otherwise would fester and some practical action steps should come out of it. What do you think?"

If the client buys into "what" you are recommending but has concerns about the "how," negotiation is necessary and desirable. An example of a negotiating statement is:

- "What's important to you about the teambuilding? What's important to me is that we surface the team members' concerns. What if you and I together develop a list of issues to discuss and get feedback on it from the team?

We could also do the teambuilding in two sessions so that you and I have a chance to digest the team's comments. What do you think?"

Confronting

Confronting is the consulting response if there is No Action. Confronting is usually needed when the client has verbally agreed with a goal or action item and has appeared to be "sold," but no action has occurred. By his or her lack of action, without using words, the client is saying, "I don't buy this," or "This isn't worth my time." The consultant must surface the resistance, listen, then respond with one of the other skills. Examples of Confronting statements are:

- "You seem reluctant to start collecting data."
- "You've missed your last three action items."
- "You seem skeptical about the value of mapping out this process."
- "You seem concerned about bringing this up with the team."

Solving

Solving is the consulting response if there is No Success. The client has implemented the recommendations of the past and encountered a problem. In this case, the consultant must join the client in analyzing the situation and in developing a solution. Conceptual models (such as force-field analysis) and problem-solving tools (such as fishbone diagrams and brainstorming) may be helpful. Examples of Solving statements are:

- "What do you feel the problem is?"
- "What does the team feel the problem is?"
- "What would have to happen for this to work?"
- "Let's consider some other alternatives..."

<u>R</u>ecord

Closing on action means summarizing the solution, closing on specific action steps, and planning follow-up. The consultant should have a record of the content and action forward of each consulting contact. Examples of Recording statements are:

- "Let me see if I can summarize what we came up with..."
- "What should I write down as our solution?"
- "What needs to be done to implement this?"
- "How can I help in this?"
- "It looks like an action item for you is to share the list of possible performance measures with the team. It looks like an action item for me is to get some examples of what similar teams are measuring."

Consulting At The Team Level

Consulting at the team level usually involves helping teams in three areas:

1. Facilitation
2. Team development
3. Team effectiveness

Facilitation means guiding teams in discussion, drawing-out participants' comments and organizing them. Team development, also called teambuilding, involves developing the group dynamics and maturation level of the team. Team effectiveness refers to the practical organizational skills by which the team operates on a day-to-day basis, such as problem-solving, decision-making, planning, and team meetings.

The consultant can use a checklist or model, survey, interviews, or observation to determine how best to help a team. Several team checklists are included in *Continuous Improvement: Teams & Tools*. Figure 7.4 shows a simple tool for gathering team member input about areas for team improvement. In this situation, team members rate each area as having primary priority for improvement, secondary priority, or as being O.K. Useful models for assessing a team's current state include the Stages of Team Development and the Building Blocks of Team Effectiveness (see Chapter 3).

Facilitation

Facilitation means making something easier. In group dynamics, facilitation means helping a team discuss and resolve an issue itself. A good facilitator elicits and organizes the input of all involved. The goals of a facilitator are to: 1) listen and draw out participation, 2) handle emotions raised during the discussion, 3) keep the discussion productive and on the topic, and 4) guide the discussion to some decision.

A facilitator provides objectivity, structure, and an action orientation. Objectivity comes from the fresh perspective provided by the facilitator. Structure refers to an organized approach to discussing a topic. A team facing a complex issue can benefit from looking at it according to a particular conceptual model. Sometimes the model itself is less important than simply having an organized approach. An action orientation means that the facilitator prompts the team to resolve an issue, a plan, and take specific action.

A good facilitator identifies what specific facilitative role to play with each team. Some teams are ready to talk and just need someone to capture

	Primary	Secondary	OK
1. Increasing Customer Focus/Feedback			
2. Increasing Timeliness & Responsiveness			
3. Better Use of Resources			
4. Increasing Cost-Effectiveness			
5. Eliminating Unnecessary Activities			
6. Better Follow-up on Suggestions & Problems			
7. Lowest Level Decisions & Authority			
8. Clearer Definition of Goals & Mission			
9. Rewarding & Recognizing Performance			
10. Better Meetings			
11. Measuring & Feedback on Performance			
12. More Emphasis on Team Concept			
13. More Emphasis on Training			
14. Better Communication & Flow of Information			
15. Minimizing Red Tape & Bureaucracy			
16. Eliminating Bottlenecks in Work Flow			

Figure 7.4 Target Areas for Improvement

their thoughts. Others are silent and need a questioner. Others are stuck and need an idea person. Some get off the track and require a strong gatekeeper.

Facilitation Skills

Facilitation skills are an extension of reflective listening skills (see Chapter 3) and include prompting by name, rephrasing, relating comments, and gatekeeping.

Prompting by name. Prompting by name is calling on someone who has not spoken or whose body language indicates a reaction: "Jim, I see you're nodding. How does this look from your area?"

Rephrasing the group. Rephrasing the group is sensing an overall group message and saying it back to the group for confirmation or clarification: "I hear the group saying that we need to look at how many projects each person is working on."

Relating comments. Relating comments is connecting similar comments made at different points in time, or comparing comments that appear to contradict each other. Examples are: "Mary, is John's comment an example of what you were saying earlier?" and "So far, I'm hearing Bob say that the customers need training, but I'm hearing Ann say that the team itself needs training."

Gatekeeping the discussion. Gatekeeping is keeping the discussion on-track. Tools for gatekeeping include a set of ground rules, an issues list, and a team action record.

Agenda. An agenda with time-frames is the primary gatekeeping tool. The facilitator may want to assign a timekeeper to keep one eye on the clock and one eye on the agenda. The timekeeper announces how much time the agenda allows for each topic, and prompts the team when that time is completed. The team then moves on, or continues the discussion by removing or shortening another agenda item.

Ground Rules. Ground rules are the team's code of conduct, in other words, how team members will act toward each other. Ground rules should be posted at the start of the meeting, and the facilitator should point out any violations of the ground rules during the meeting. Sample ground rules include:

1. Baby new ideas.
2. Give a headline before detail.
3. Draw out others' ideas before giving your own.
4. Complete all commitments to the team.
5. Frankness will rule during meetings.

Issues list. An issues list (also called a concerns list or parking lot) is a posted list on which the facilitator records important but off-the-topic items so that an issue is captured but the group can stay on-track. The facilitator may want to assign an issues recorder to maintain the list and reintroduce issues until they are resolved.

Team action record. The team action record lists all agreed-upon actions and decisions, in other words, who is going to do what and by when. The facilitator may assign an action recorder to log all team action items. The action recorder should be vigorous in recording action by the name of the person responsible and the time promised.

The facilitator should be assertive about calling attention to an agenda item, referring an item to the issues list, or pointing out a relevant ground rule. Helpful gatekeeping phrases are:

- "Time out."
- "Let's get back on-track."

- "I'm aware of time, so I'd like to use the remaining time in the following way..."

Tips On Facilitation

1. Raise an issue as your own: "A concern I have is..." or, "Something I'm aware of is..." or, "Something I wonder about is..."

2. Get discussion going by asking about pro's and con's: "What do you see as the benefits of this?" and "What concerns or risks do you see?"

3. Don't be too personal or confrontive when asking questions for group participation. "What concerns do you feel people have?" is easier to answer than, "What concerns do you have?"

4. Don't flinch at negative comments.

5. Rephrase often: "What you are saying is..." Reinforce all, or at least most, of the group's comments, especially in the beginning of the discussion: "That's interesting," or, "Good point," or "I hadn't thought of that."

6. Reassure people about what will be done with information, opinions, or ideas they offer: "I'll pass your comments along as coming from this group, but without using individual names."

7. If the group is somewhat large or the topic is a difficult or emotional one, try dividing into smaller groups for an initial discussion. The contents of the small-group discussions can then be shared with the large group.

8. Use the body language of good listening: eye contact, nodding, facing the speaker, leaning slightly toward the speaker, and matching facial expressions to the content of the speaker's statement.

9. Connect statements to other statements made earlier: "That goes back to what John said before about..."

10. Write key words and comments on a flipchart or blackboard.

The Team Meeting

To improve a team's effectiveness, watch it in action. Since it is usually difficult to observe a team doing its actual work, a team is most accessible to a consultant in its meetings. We believe that the best way to improve team effectiveness is to help a team conduct regular team meetings. The team meeting is a critical element of a total team system. A team system cannot operate successfully unless all teams are having effective team meetings. A team meeting is different from a typical staff meeting. The agenda of a team meeting has a particular format (see Figure 7.5) The elements of a team meeting are:

- *Review of the agenda and past action items* — The team holds itself accountable for commitments from the previous meeting.
- *Information sharing* — News, upcoming events, and technical information are shared.
- *Performance review* — Key measures of progress are reviewed.
- *Recognition* — Accomplishments and cooperation are recognized.
- *Problem-solving, process focus, or team learning* — The team addresses a current problem, analyzes a process, or has a mini-lesson.
- *Action planning* — The team reviews and documents who is going to do what by when (see Figure 7.6).
- *Next agenda* — Topics for the next meeting are identified.

Coaching A Team On Meetings

Coaching a team on meetings involves assisting with preparation, observing, and giving feedback.

Team Meeting Agenda

Team: _____ Team Leader: _____

Date/Place: _____Notetaker: _____

Team Members Present:_____

_____

I.   **Review Agenda.** [_____ mins]

II.   **Review Team Action Record.** [_____ mins]

III.   **Information Sharing.** [_____ mins]

IV.   **Performance Review.** [_____ mins]

V.   **Recognition.** [_____ mins]

VI.   **Problem-Solving / Process Focus / Team Learning** [_____ mins]

VII.   **Action Planning.** [_____ mins]

VIII. **Next Agenda.** [_____ mins]

Figure 7.5 A Team Meeting Agenda Form

Team Action Record

Team_____ Date_____

Who	What	When	Done

Figure 7.6 A Team Action Record Form

Assisting with preparation. To help a team leader prepare for a team meeting, meet together beforehand to prepare the meeting agenda. Decide the content and timing of each section. What items will be addressed in each section of the agenda? How much time will be spent on each part of the agenda? Will roles such as timekeeper and action recorder be assigned? Will any section of the agenda be facilitated by someone other than the team leader? What points of information should be shared? What points should be made about the latest performance data? What recognition to the team or an individual should be shared?

Team Meeting Observation Sheet

Level 4: Involvement

____Team problem-solving and team decision-making occurred with all team members participating.

____At least half of the team discussion was "proactive" and "anticipatory."

Level 3: Content

____Team discussed progress on each of its critical objectives, including specific action plans.

____Some team problem-solving and team decision-making occurred.

Level 2: Mechanics

____Reviewed agenda at the start of the meeting and followed it throughout.

____Team discussed its progress on action plans.

____Leader used open-ended questions, prompting, and other listening skills to get participation.

____Leader kept the meeting on track by keeping people on task, handling disruptions, resolving disagreements, etc.

____Leader followed-up on people's action steps from previous meetings.

____Leader used positive reinforcement.

____Someone took notes as minutes of the meeting.

____Team answered the questions: "What did we decide? Who's going to do what by when?"

Level 1: Needs Improvement

____Agenda not reviewed or followed.

____Team did not discuss progress on action plans.

____Minimal participation; leader talked the most.

____Meeting got off track.

____Little or no follow-up of previous action steps.

____Little or no positive reinforcement.

____No notes taken as minutes.

____No discussion or recording of: "What did we decide? Who's going to do what by when?"

Figure 7.7 Team Meeting Observation Sheet

Observation. Observe the team meeting as an unobtrusive guest. Use a team meeting observation sheet to organize your notes and structure your feedback (see Figure 7.7).

Feedback. Both the team as a whole and the team leader individually should receive feedback. To coach the team as a whole, provide several points of positive and developmental feedback about the team's interactions at the end of the meeting.

To provide individual feedback to the team leader, start by asking, "How do you feel the team meeting went?" It is important for the team leader to learn to observe his or her own behavior and that of the team. Build on the team leader's comments.

To offer your own feedback, focus on the positive first. Recognize small improvements if necessary. Don't overwhelm the team leader with observations. Summarize your feedback in key points:

- "Something that I thought you did well was to ask if there were data available on the problem of excessive rush orders."

Add developmental feedback. Translate your feedback into action for next time:

- "Something you could have done differently would be to get the team to help you define the exact problem with rush orders, then get two or three people to do a fishbone diagram for the next meeting."

- "One thing that may work better for you is to get the team members handling some part of the agenda so that the meeting is not so dependent on you. Why not have a different person review the performance data at each meeting?"

Designing New Systems As A Deliverable

Designing new systems is a key deliverable for change agents because the performance of the organization is ultimately determined by people acting in habitual roles, following formal or informal policies, using existing tools, and operating established processes. Those roles, policies, tools, and processes must be redesigned to support any change. To make change permanent, the consultant must help groups throughout the organization design systems that optimize the combined technical and social systems. In designing new systems, the consultant must make sure that design charters are fully developed and well-understood, must assure that thorough design methodology is applied, and must encourage fresh, unconventional thinking during the design process (see Chapter 8.)

"Change the environment; do not try to change man."

R. Buckminster Fuller,

American architect and engineer

Design Skills

Design skills that are essential for the consultant are:

- Picturing the vision, mission, and principles
- Initial planning and implementation planning
- Facilitation
- Process thinking, process mapping, and process analysis
- Perspective, creativity, and judgment
- Knowledge of design principles

- Familiarity with the organization's structure, systems, and skill base
- Being a cultural observer

Picturing The Vision, Mission, And Principles

The consultant must be able to picture the vision, mission, and principles put into practice and imagine their implications for the business and for the organization as a mini-society.

Initial Planning

The consultant must be able to guide the creation of a charter for system or process design. The charter defines the objectives, scope, and boundaries of the design. A key objective, might be to "cut all delivery times in half." The scope might be "all processes from order to cash, and all operations and functions in this division." A boundary might be that "existing physical facilities must be retained."

Facilitation

Design is usually accomplished by design teams, that is, groups representing a "diagonal slice" of the organization, whose members are experts in their areas, creative, and constructively dissatisfied. The design teams' task is to "start from scratch and blueprint" the ideal system. Such groups must be guided, listened to, and challenged.

Process Thinking

Redesigning a system requires identifying: a) suppliers, customers, and other key stakeholders, b) inputs and outputs, and c) processes within the system. The most critical processes and the right level of detail must be determined. Assuming that 20% of the processes produce 80% of the problems in a system, the consultant must help a design team target the most appropriate processes and determine the right level of analytical detail.

Process Mapping

The consultant must be able to lead a design team in picturing "how the work gets done now." The consultant must help the design team draw maps of how, where, and to whom the work flows.

Process Analysis

Once a design team has "papered the walls" with current-state maps, the consultant must be able to help the team "walk through them" analytically. The consultant must help the team identify duplications of effort, bottlenecks, repetition of steps, inspection points, decision points, excessive handling, communication gaps, overspecialization, senseless procedures, and pointless policies.

Perspective, Creativity, And Judgment

The consultant must be able to help the team generate ideas for a new system. The consultant may facilitate the team's use of creativity and problem-solving techniques, such as brainstorming and "what-if" exercises.

Knowledge Of Design Principles

Design principles include: a) organize around outcomes, not tasks, b) have those who use the output perform the process, c) build information-processing work into the actual work that produces the information, d) link parallel activities instead of integrating their results, e) put decisions where the work is performed to build control into the process, and f) capture information once, at its source. The consultant must be familiar with these and other design principles (see Lynch and Werner, 1994).

Familiarity With The Organization's Structure

Designing new systems is likely to have implications for the organization's structure, from the primary work teams up, including levels, spans of control, grouping, and functionality, ratios of managers to non-managers, and decision-making authorities at each level. The consultant must be familiar with the logic and workings of the present structure and be able to imagine new structures.

Familiarity With The Organization's Systems

Systems that may be directly and indirectly affected by new designs include: communications, feedback, planning and budgeting, decision-making, information, recognition, hiring, training, appraisal, promotion, and compensation systems. The consultant must understand how these systems work and their strengths, weaknesses, and interdependencies.

Familiarity With The Organization's Skill Base

Skills that may be designed into the organization include interpersonal and team skills, technical skills, multiple-job skills, business skills, and general education. The consultant must be familiar with how skills are currently trained and evaluated, and must be able to envision entire new skill sets.

Being A Cultural Observer

New designs of systems and processes often have implications for the style and symbols of the organization. Style refers to habitual interpersonal behavior, including management style and behavior with customers. Symbols are the physical and social cues in the organization that prompt specific behavior in the members of the organization. The consultant must be a cultural observer, with enough of an outside perspective to be able to spot styles and symbols, describe them, and consider their appropriateness to the new design.

Implementation Planning

The output of process and system designs are technical and social changes that must be made. The consultant must be able to assist in identifying how they will be made, by when, and by whom. This includes participating in priority-setting — which changes should be made immediately and which changes require a long-term approach.

Summary

In this chapter we have addressed the four basic deliverables of a consultant: communication, training, coaching, and designing new systems. In the next chapter, we will cover the three basic approaches to organizational improvement.

8

Three Approaches To Change

Reengineering Processes And People Systems

Targeted Process Improvement

Total Team Systems

Three Approaches To Change

The approach of a change effort refers to its organizing set of principles and techniques. The client and consultant must collaboratively decide which approach (or approaches) will provide the theoretical underpinnings of their effort. Today, there are three basic approaches to change, each with advantages and potential pitfalls. A clear understanding of each approach and its implications is essential for planning successful organizational improvement.

The objectives of this chapter are to describe the three basic approaches to organizational improvement and offer guidelines for implementing each. The consultant should be able to describe the features, benefits, and steps of each approach and help the client distinguish and decide among them.

The three main approaches to organizational improvement are: reengineering business processes and people systems, targeted process improvement, and total team systems. *Reengineering business processes and people systems* means radically redesigning processes, as well as the organization itself, to optimize quality, cost, and speed. Processes and people systems are jointly optimized. *Targeted process improvement* means improving a key process that cuts across the functions of the organization. Usually a steering team charters a process improvement team to analyze a process and make recommendations for redesign. A *total team system* means that everyone is on a team, and that the business is operated through teams. Teams use performance data, the tools of quality, problem-solving and decision-making skills, and team meetings to operate processes to meet customer requirements. Let's examine the steps of each approach in more detail.

Reengineering Business Processes And People Systems

Reengineering business processes and people systems attempts to "blow everything up and start over," recreating a "green-field" experience when all aspects of the organization are "built from scratch." This approach is distinguished from the other approaches by the "outrageous objective" and the belief that "we can't there from here." An "outrageous objective" is one that seems impossible today, such as reducing manufacturing costs by 20%. If it seems impossible, it is because significant constraints are built into the basic processes, systems, and policies of the organization. The basic structure and functioning of the organization prevents large improvement. Reengineering examines that basic structure and the way it functions.

The Steps In Reengineering

The steps in redesigning the processes and people systems in the organization are depicted in Figure 8.1.

1. Define The Future

Defining the future involves identifying opportunities and challenges and determining current capability.

Identifying opportunities and challenges. The interplay of three planning activities identifies opportunities and challenges (see Chapter 5).

"Outside-in" analysis assesses the events and trends in the external environment and a set of future scenarios. "Inside-out" analysis evaluates the capability of work processes. Organizational analysis defines the human environment, or people systems, that support the processes and create the fabric we call "culture."

Current Capability. Capability refers to the present ability of the

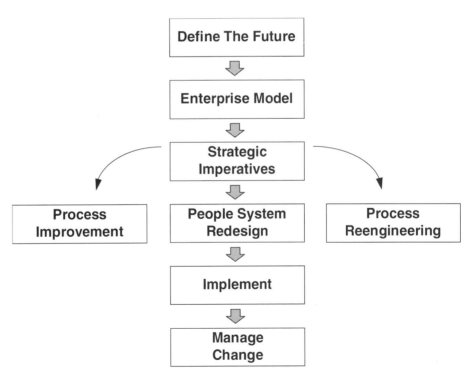

Figure 8.1 The Steps in Reengineering Business Processes and People Systems

organization to accomplish work. This means quantifying the performance of the major processes of the organization. Capability can be a strategic asset (sometimes referred to as "marketable know-how") or a strategic liability if the organization needs to do things it cannot do. Reengineering should proceed if defining the future indicates the need for an "outrageous objective" and current capability shows that "we can't get there from here."

2. Develop An Enterprise Model

A new picture of the organization should be drawn to break old paradigms that defined past success. A process view of the business replaces the traditional organization chart. This view should show how work really flows across the organization. The enterprise model is concerned with the "what" of work, not how it is accomplished or by whom. The enterprise model of the business distills the complexity of the organization to a set of basic processes. Before developing an enterprise model of the organization it is helpful to identify the kinds of processes that are typical in an organization.

Core organizational processes. Core organizational processes are the large-scale, fundamental processes that represent the mission of the organization. Core organizational processes, such as new product development or order delivery, hold the greatest opportunity for improvement for three reasons. First, virtually every team and individual can influence these processes. Second, since a core organizational process usually does not fall within functional boundaries, it often goes unstudied in its entirety. Third, organizational barriers often make the workings of a core organizational process very convoluted.

Standard processes. Standard processes are processes that everyone in an organization should do the same way. Plans for such processes can be disseminated throughout an organization to minimize unnecessary variation and "reinventing the wheel." Standard processes can include "people" processes (such as hiring, recognition, appraisal, and salary administration), administrative processes (such as ordering and invoicing), and common work processes (such as planning, budgeting, and project management). The opportunity to improve standard processes is enormous. In some organizations there are literally dozens of ways of managing projects, doing budgets, and writing reports. The need for standardization and consistency is clear.

New processes. New processes are processes being started from scratch as a result of a new product, customer, or technology. The process approach asks questions such as: What is the definition of the process? Who is the process owner? Is there a team aligned around the process? Who are the suppliers and what are their inputs to the process? Who are the customers of the process and what are their requirements for the process output? How will the process be measured and managed? What are the causes of process and output variation, and how will they be controlled?

3. Mobilize For Change

Mobilize for change means deciding "what we should work on," and beginning the effort. The choices are: 1) end-to-end processes to reengineer, 2) contained processes to improve, and 3) people systems to redesign. End-to-end processes are processes that cross the entire organization from external supplier to external customer. Everything about the process, including its boundaries and the form of its inputs and outputs, may be radically reconceptualized. Contained processes are work processes within an end-to-end process. The operation of a contained process is analyzed to improve its quality, cost, and speed.

After deciding what to work on, the task of the steering team is to:
- Define the objectives, scope, and boundaries of the project.
- Set time-frames and resources.
- Select and train one or more design teams.
- Communicate to the organization.
- Establish milestones and progress reviews.

4. Improve, Reengineer, And Redesign

In Step 4, the work of process improvement, process reengineering, and people systems redesign is done.

Process improvement. Process improvement identifies better ways of operating contained processes (see the next section on Targeted Process Improvement).

Process reengineering. The most profound element of reengineering methodology is re-conceptualizing the fundamental nature of the work. To re-conceptualize the work one must ask some basic questions:
- Can we do without this work altogether?
- Can we combine the work in a way that changes what we do?
- Can we redefine the work?

- Can we move key aspects of the work upstream to suppliers or downstream to customers to add value and take out cost?
- Can we redefine the boundaries of the process to create an end-to-end process?
- Can we collapse the time required to do the work by bringing together the elements of the whole process, eliminating waiting and moving time?

People systems redesign. Since processes are operated by human beings, people systems must be part of any redesign. Examples of people systems that are common to the organization are:
- Reward and recognition
- Evaluation
- Compensation
- Policies

People systems that are unique to a process that has undergone reengineering or improvement must be redesigned to support it. These people systems are likely to include:
- Job design
- Team configuration
- Management roles and levels
- Information requirements

5. Plan And Implement

The transition from design to implementation is treacherous. Many reengineering projects are unsuccessful. Some common causes of failure are:

- Design teams are disbanded after plans are approved, leaving implementation teams disconnected from the design team's original thinking.

- Design teams and leadership teams evolve significantly during the design experience and become impatient with the rest of the organization.

- Associates are not given enough details of process operation and reject the new designs.

- Team leaders are not trained in the new philosophy and skills.

- The role of internal consultant is not sufficiently fulfilled.

- Leaders do not drive the implementation to completion.

6. Manage Change

Communicate about the implementation efforts through all of the regular communication channels in the organization (see Chapter 7). Keep in mind the "7 x 7 rule" — communicate the message seven times in seven different ways. Communicate progress about both activities and results. Use all types of organization-wide publications and meetings. Communication should include positive recognition for all progress.

Targeted Process Improvement

Targeted process improvement means focusing on a key process that cuts across the functions of the organization. The expectation of targeted process improvement is that process performance will be dramatically improved, although the fundamental social environment will not be addressed in the process analysis. This does not mean that changes in social systems cannot be made. In fact, it is likely that systems related to the process, such as decision-making, training, and accountability, will be changed. It simply means that the design team does not expect to create a new work environment.

When To Use Targeted Process Improvement

Define, measure, and improve your work process if it:

- Does not deliver products or services desired by the customer.
- Produces variable and unpredictable results (in quality, cost, or speed).
- Has no flexibility against customer expectations and requirements.
- Does not produce what the customer wants or expects.
- Adds no value for the customer.
- Is done by people without the necessary skills or information.
- Creates rework.
- Is done with inadequate or misused equipment.

The Steps In Targeted Process Improvement

The steps in process improvement are:

1. Define the process.
2. Identify customer requirements.
3. Map the current state.
4. Analyze the process.
5. Identify improvements.
6. Map the ideal state and implement.
7. Establish a management process.

1. Define The Process

At this initial step in process improvement, the process itself must be defined. Process definition involves defining:

- The process output.
- The name of the process.
- The beginning and ending points of the process.
- The customers of the process.
- The inputs to the process.
- The suppliers of input to the process.

Begin process definition by completing a worksheet like the one in Figure 8.2.

After completing the initial definition of the process, the team should check to be sure that the process is being addressed in the most holistic fashion possible. Can the boundaries be stretched upstream or downstream to include other activities that would make a whole process?

2. Identify Customer Requirements

Once the process has been well-defined it is essential to understand the

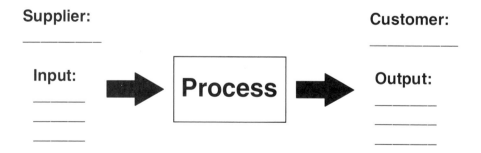

Figure 8.2 A Process Definition Worksheet

customer's requirements of the outputs of the process. Requirements should define quality and service from the customer's perspective. Requirements should be written from the perspective of the customer and written in language that customers would really use. Avoid technical jargon. Requirements are usually defined in terms of the cost, quality, speed, and service expectations of the customer. Identify customer requirements by completing a worksheet like the one in Figure 8.3.

3. Map The Current State

Process mapping is the technique of using flowcharts to illustrate the flow of a process, proceeding from the most macro perspective to the level of detail

Supplier: _____

Input: _____
_____
_____

Process

Customer: _____

Output: _____
_____
_____

Process Requirements:
_____
_____
_____
_____
_____

Customer Requirements:
_____
_____
_____
_____
_____

Figure 8.3 A Customer Requirement Worksheet

required to identify opportunities for improvement. The purpose of this step is to map, but not memorialize, the current state. As you map the current state, be aware of the pitfalls of digging into the "as is" process. Usually a five- or six-step macro map will provide sufficient detail to identify process problems and stimulate improvement ideas. More detail is only helpful when team members have difficulty coming up with improvement ideas.

Macro process maps. A macro flowchart, or macro process map, illustrates the major steps of the process. The single box is exploded into several boxes. The example in Figure 8.4 shows a macro map of a hiring process. In this case, the hiring process has three macro steps. A process

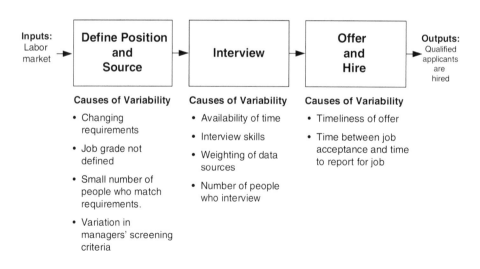

Figure 8.4 A Macro Process Map of Hiring

definition worksheet (Figure 8.2) and a customer requirements worksheet (Figure 8.3) should accompany a macro map.

Relationship maps. If a number of teams and individuals touch the process, use a relationship map to identify the hand-offs. A relationship map (Figure 8.5) shows *who* performs each step in the process. Relationship maps can dramatically illustrate illogical aspects of a process, such as unnecessary movements or the poorly-timed involvement of an individual or group.

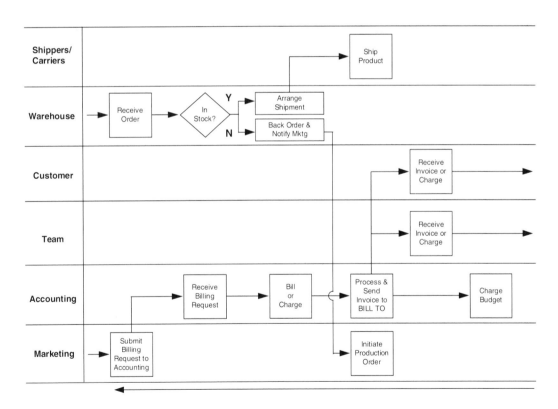

Figure 8.5 A Section of a Relationship Map

Some tips for process mapping are:

1. Focus only on the work, not on who does it or how it is done.

2. Map how the process operates 80% of the time without accounting for all of the exceptions.

3. When in doubt, go for less rather than more detail. Make sure that the big picture is clear before diving into details.

4. Analyze The Process

Once the current state has been mapped, analysis of the process can begin. In process analysis, we want to know what is less-than-ideal about the process in terms of inherent variability, construction, cost, and most importantly, capability to produce output that meets and exceeds customer requirements. The design team should ask, "Why do we do this? How do we know if we're doing this right? Do we need to do this at all?"

5. Identify Improvements

Identify ways of redesigning the process, controlling variability, and measuring process performance. The design team should use common sense, creativity, knowledge of technology, and information about the best practices to develop a set of design recommendations.

6. Map The Ideal Process And Implement

Present the redesigned process to the steering team. After approval, present the new design to all of the teams involved. Develop specific action steps. If necessary, form an implementation team to assist in putting the new process into place.

7. Establish A Management Process

Design methods of collecting and displaying data about the process and its outputs. Develop and communicate procedures and responsibilities for operating the process. Determine how to handle excessive variability in the process when it occurs. Proceed with the implementation.

Total Team Systems

The traditional organization chart has emphasized the boss-subordinate relationship and the organization of people around common functions. This vertical-functional organization has become completely dysfunctional today. The reality of organizations is that work is accomplished across the organization. Historically, the inefficiency and ineffectiveness of "crossing-the-moat" between functions was built into profit margins as a cost of doing business.

In the vertical organization, a "silo effect" is created because communication and concerns flow up and down the silo. In the silo-based organization, the main test of quality is whether the boss, or the boss's boss, will buy it. The output of work performed in a silo is shipped to the next silo and forgotten. Communication often emanates at the process level and is funneled to the top where top-to-top communication occurs with little or no communication between the first-level customer and supplier. This causes a "telephone effect" where the message deteriorates in the multiple repetitions required to get the word to someone who can act. The silo effect and the telephone effect work to create independence and antagonism where there should be interdependence and cooperation.

A total team system turns the vertical organization on its side. The result is a horizontal organization that emphasizes the fundamental work relationships between suppliers and internal customers. The boss becomes a process owner and a coach to process operators. Managers, in the role of coach, learn to become value-adding suppliers to the process operators.

The implications for structure are significant. When we think from the customer backward and think in terms of core processes that produce products and services for customers, we can imagine vastly different structures. Sales and service, for example, are not separated into warring functions, but are formed into teams around the customer service process.

In order to avoid the silo effect and facilitate timely and accurate communication, it is important to look at how work is accomplished from the horizontal perspective. Figure 8.6 is a representation of the horizontal organization. Each triangle represents an individual team. The boxes represent the processes that each team operates. The responsibilities of a team match the boundaries of the processes it operates. Each team has essential relationships with the other teams. Each team receives input from teams "upstream" in the process flow (its suppliers) and operates its processes to produce outputs for teams "downstream" (its customers). The role of a leadership team is to provide the teams with what they need to operate their processes to serve their customers.

These work processes, woven together by internal customer and supplier partnerships, form a chain of customer service. Providing customer service that is truly distinctive depends upon the ability to work seamlessly behind the scenes and execute flawlessly for the customer.

New organizational structures emerge based on a process definition of "team." A series of functional teams that hand off work to the next functional team in line may be more effective as a set of multi-functional teams, each with all of the skills necessary to produce complete products and services.

Teams As A System

A team system is formed when individual teams are bonded with other

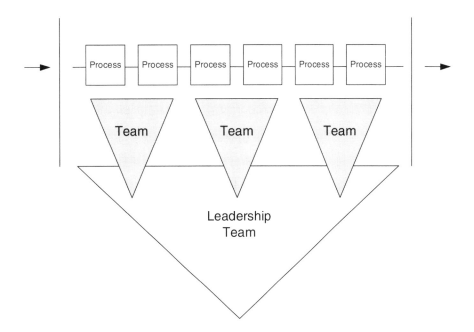

Figure 8.6 The Horizontal Organization

teams in the organization as links in the customer-supplier chain. Each team seeks to optimize the capability of its work process and deliver on its performance promise. Seamless execution is achieved when every team has a dynamic partnership with every other team upon which it depends. Unfortunately, teams can exist throughout an organization without ever becoming a *system* of teams. There is great power when a collection of teams are forged into a whole greater than the sum of its parts.

In a team system, everyone is a part of a team, and each team has the responsibility for improving its performance continuously. The characteristics of a team system are:

- Teams are organized around business processes.
- Each action of the team adds value.
- Teams are linked across the organization by customer and supplier partnerships.
- Teams are guided by a common mission and focus on the customer.

A team system redefines the traditional chain-of-command. Communication patterns in a team system need not follow the traditional hierarchical lines. Communication is governed by the interdependent working relationships among teams. Speed of communication is accelerated because teams talk directly with their customers and suppliers.

Natural Work Teams

There are two ways to structure the teams of the organization. The first is to accept the structure as it is and organize people into teams based on current relationships to supervisors and managers. This structure is an effective first step in forming a team-based organization. Essential skills are learned and interdependencies between teams are established in terms of supplier and customer partnerships. Over time, the opportunity to rethink the organization's structure, based on core organizational processes, can be pursued.

A second way to organize teams is to redefine the team structure from the outset along process lines. This requires a thoughtful analysis of the primary processes of the business, and development of the skill set required to operate the process. In either case, a permanent structure of teams is required to optimize the use of quality improvement skills and tools.

Process Improvement Teams

Process improvement teams are an important complement to the natural team structure. The units of any organization, even one with the most process-based team structure, will be highly interdependent. Process improvement teams take members from different teams or process ownership groups and assign them the task of improving a whole process.

Summary

In this chapter, we have examined three approaches to organizational improvement: reengineering business processes and people systems, targeted process improvement, and total team systems. In the next chapter, we will cover ways of responding to resistance to change.

9

Understanding Resistance To Change

9

Helping Someone Face Change

Responding To Initial Resistance

Responding To Learned Resistance

Consultant Resistance

Understanding Resistance To Change

Everyone knows that change is difficult and people resist it. Handling resistance to change is a fundamental challenge of leaders and consultants.

The purpose of this chapter is to describe how to help people handle change and how to respond to resistance to change.

Helping Someone Face Change

People in the midst of change undergo a significant psychological experience. How should a change agent help someone facing change?

Realize What The Person Is Going Through

We shouldn't argue with people's feelings during change or be surprised by their strong reactions. Changes cause losses of identity — and it is the losses, not the changes themselves (or the consultants), that people are reacting to. A person in the midst of change is being forced to say good-bye to a part of his or her self. This is true whether the person initiated the change or not, and whether the change is perceived as positive or not. Consultants should not scoff at people who are struggling with change. As William Bridges, in *Managing Transitions: Making the Most of Change,* points out: "It's a piece of their world that is being lost, not ours — we often react the same way when it's part of ourselves that is being lost."

Talk It Through

Robert Carkcuff, in *The Art of Helping VI,* offers us a useful model for a one-to-one helping discussion. Although the counselor-type role in Carkcuff's model may not fit your situation exactly, the concepts and use of skills are instructive.

Carkhuff notes that for the change to begin the client must first be *involved.* The consultant engages the client's involvement through attending — listening and showing interest. The consultant uses active listening skills, noting common themes, intensity of expression, and repetitions, and being sensitive to the person's movements, expressions, and posture. Empathy, respect, and warmth are essential.

As the client becomes involved, the consultant responds, helping the person explore and assess his or her current situation. The consultant tries to connect the content of the statements with the feelings expressed, for example, "You feel frustrated because of all the new emphasis on teams." The consultant's goal is to help the client be specific about what's happening and how he or she feels about it: "You feel concerned because the reengineering effort is asking for such huge improvements."

The consultant then works to "personalize" the client's exploration, helping the client transform the problems into goals. The client has to come to an understanding of the personal implications of the change. The client must also take responsibility of transforming problems into goals. The consultant's response can evolve from *connecting the client's feelings to external factors:* "You feel frustrated because of all the new emphasis on teams," to *connecting the change effort to abstract feelings possessed by the client:* "You feel frustrated because you don't feel comfortable in the team meeting format." Finally, the consultant must *connect positive feelings to action:* "You feel ready to learn about team meeting skills." Confrontation may be necessary: "On the one hand, I hear you saying that the company has to change, but on the other hand, you haven't participated in any of the change efforts."

Wording will vary and active listening should be used in-between, but an organizational improvement consultant might apply Carkhuff's personalizing sequence in this way:

- "You feel concerned because the reengineering effort is asking for such huge improvements." *(the client's feelings are connected to outside factors)*
- "You feel concerned because you don't see where the improvements can come from." *(the client's feelings are connected to personal factors)*
- "You feel concerned because you aren't familiar yet with the reengineering methodology." *(the clients' feelings are connected to the gaps between the client's current situation and the goal)*
- "You feel interested in attending the reengineering team training." *(the client's positive feelings are connected to the goal)*

After defining the goal, the consultant initiates action planning, helping the client develop specific action steps. The plans must be specific enough that the client can *act* on them and progress can be clearly marked.

- "The first step is to sign up for the training."

- "The next steps will be to identify a process for reengineering and to determine how your team can participate."

Feedback to the client on progress is important:
- "Something that you're doing that really helps is bringing up real-world situations in the training."
- "One thing that may help would be to identify processes that are important and that can be influenced by your team."

Help The Person Sort Out What's Going On

> *"In a time of turbulence and change, it is more true than ever that knowledge is power."*
> *John F. Kennedy*

Bridges offers some suggestions for helping people understand what a change really means. A key step is to provide information about the "who, what, when, where, why, and how" of the change over and over (a good rule of thumb previously mentioned is "7 x 7" — say it seven times in seven different ways). Help the client define the change. What is actually going to change? What is the client going to have to let go of? The converse is also important — identify the continuities, that is, what is not changing but continuing on.

Expect Grief

As consultants, we should expect and give the signs of grieving: shock, denial, anger, bargaining, anxiety, and sadness. We must be able to acknowledge losses openly and sympathetically. For example: "Having to increase speed and cut costs at the same time seems impossible. It puts us in the situation of questioning every single thing we do, and that's uncomfortable." "Having to compete for business that we used to get automatically will make most of us feel anxious and pressured. I feel that way myself." Treat the past with respect; don't ridicule the old way. Since people identify with the old way, making fun of it is making fun of them.

Expect A Period Of Confusion

People go through a "neutral zone" after they leave something behind (see Chapter 1). Don't be surprised by a phase of the "blah's." Expect a period of anxiety, resentment, lack of motivation, and even illness as people cross the gap from the old to the new. Communicate often during this phase, continue to describe the change in a positive light, and prepare to monitor performance closely.

Expect Resistance

Peter Block has said, "Resistance is nature's way of telling you that something important is going on." In *The Transformational Leader,* Noel M. Tichy and Mary Anne Devanna have described several types of resistance to change. Inertia is the resistance of those who have always done things one way and who have trouble changing those habits. Fear of the unknown is the anxiety that goes with an unpredictable future. Sunk cost, or prior investment, in the old ways may make change hard to accept. Change may threaten power, make resources scarce, or indict past actions. Cultural values may produce selective perception, making it hard to see new ways.

Daryl Conner, in *Managing at the Speed of Change: How Resilient Managers Succeed and Prosper Where Others Fail,* notes that we seem more comfortable with change when our ability and willingness to change can help determine the outcome of events. Resistance comes from disruption of expectations. When perceived reality doesn't match expectations, the feeling of control is lost and people must adjust to changes they were unprepared for. Resistance to change occurs when people believe they have lost control over some important aspect of their lives. Whether the change is seen as positive or negative, when people's expectations are significantly disrupted, resistance occurs.

Empathize

Be sure that the resistance is not occurring because you are being obtuse, insensitive, or glib. Accurate rephrasing and empathy (see Chapter 3) are necessary to establish a foundation of authentic concern: "I hear you saying that in reengineering we could end up eliminating our own jobs. I can understand that concern."

Surface The Resistance

Peter Block suggests calmly stating the resistance that you feel: "You seem angry about how long this is taking." Empathize with the concerns that surface and reemphasize what is needed from the client for success (see Chapter 3).

Practice Sober Selling

Daryl Conner recommends using persuasion (see Chapter 3) that includes admitting the costs involved: "This reengineering effort should produce big improvements, but none of our jobs will be the same anymore."

Share Data And Facts

Resistance can be at least partially defused with data. Reactions like, "Team meetings take up all my time," and "We already know what our customers think of us without doing customer surveys," require a focus on the real facts. How much time do team meetings really take? What information exists about customer requirements and feedback?

Help Create A Vision

Without a vision, we tend to get stuck in the middle of change. The old behavior pattern doesn't work anymore, but a new pattern is not established yet. Consultants can help the client picture what it will be like to live on after the current change. To be energized, we need a vision that will pull us into the future.

Responding To Initial Resistance

When faced with resistance to change, it is useful to distinguish between initial resistance and learned resistance. Initial resistance to change is a person's negative reaction to a change when he or she first hears it described. Initial resistance is a reaction to the change message before the change itself is experienced. The best response to initial resistance is better communication.

Learned resistance to change is a person's negative reaction in the midst of a change, based on firsthand experience. Learned resistance may be to the change itself or to the way the change is being implemented. The best response to learned resistance is to analyze and improve the change effort itself.

Initial Reactions To Change

Not all initial resistance to change is stubborn or small-minded. Some resistance is sensible or at least understandable. When leaders and consultants call for change, there are several understandable reactions.

"Huh?"

This is the natural first reaction of all human beings to new messages. Anyone who has ever given instructions to a group knows this — you go over the instructions carefully, then half of the people in the room turn to the person next to them and say, "What are we supposed to do?" In this case, people aren't being resistant, they're just being human.

Leaders and consultants have to repeat their messages over and over. As Jack Welsh of GE has pointed out: "You've got to be out in front of crowds, repeating yourself over and over again, never changing your message no matter how much it bores you. You need an overarching message, something big but simple and understandable." Also, it helps to remember that words such as "quality," "value," "customer," and "process" take on huge and important connotations to believers but do not automatically have meaning to new listeners.

"You're insulting me or my past."

In other words, your message of change implies that I don't care about doing a good job, that I have not worked hard, or that I'm not a good manager. Since you don't seem to like me, I don't like your message. Obviously, consultants should not do this — don't insult people or their institutions. Don't try to invalidate anyone's past. Focus on the future and how it requires different paradigms and habits than in the past.

"Progress is impossible without change; and those who cannot change their minds cannot change anything."

George Bernard Shaw,

Anglo-Irish playwright

"I don't like to jump on bandwagons."

If your industry is fast-changing, like fashion or computers, people may be used to change. However, many of us did not grow up in an environment where it was important to get there first. We were taught to be cautious. We were told not to buy that high-tech item now — the price will come down. Remember what happened to people who bought Beta tape players! Something feels like a "bandwagon" if it seems temporary or unrelated to the "real world." Emphasize the case for action (see Chapter 7). How is the change related to the organization's strategy? What positive outcome is likely if the organization changes successfully? What negative outcome is likely if the organization does not change?

"I believe that nothing really changes."

The belief that nothing changes — the pendulum just swings back and forth — is quite common. Some people believe that if you don't like a new development, just wait because it will change back. There's some truth to this in everyday life — ties get wider and narrower, hemlines get higher and lower. But those are gentle cycles, not real changes. Point out that when fundamental paradigm shifts occur, things don't go back. We didn't swing back to hand-lettering after the printing press came along, or back to radio after television was invented.

"I just don't like these new concepts."

In other words, I don't see flowcharts, statistics, or mission statements as very useful. Maybe I have a hard time with the idea that my work is measurable, that it can be done so much faster, or that my customers' opinions should be given such weight. Perhaps I'm not used to thinking about work at all hours, or working with people of other functions, or going back to school. Discomfort with new tools and ideas is normal and understandable. As Arthur Stone Dewing wrote in *Harvard Business Review* in 1923: "The human mind welcomes the familiar. It is prejudiced in favor of that which it knows about and against that of which it is ignorant." Emphasize *trying* the new tools and techniques. Reiterate that no one has a vested interest in doing things that do not work. Support those groups who are looking for new tools and techniques.

"I don't think this is what we need."

In other words, I don't think this is the answer to our problems. I don't think that the quality of our goods, services, and processes is the problem. I don't think it's an operational or organizational problem. I think it's a strategy, marketing, or financial problem. If someone would take care of those problems, we wouldn't have to go through these changes.

First, as time passes and successes occur, the value of a change often becomes clear. As biologist James Lovelock has pointed out, "At first people say no way, then they say maybe, finally they say I knew it all the time." Second, the consultant can point out that establishing habits of data analysis, problem-solving, process management, prevention of defects, and inter-functional communication should enhance all aspects of the organization, including strategic, marketing, and financial decisions. Third, the consultant can note that, in today's world, problems cannot be compartmentalized. For example, the competitiveness of a product's costs or quality has strategic, marketing, financial, operational, and organizational implications.

"I don't like the way we're implementing this."

In other words, I don't think we need this particular type of training, survey, consulting, or whatever. This is a common and understandable reaction. While everyone might agree on the importance of customer feedback, the exact format of a customer survey and the method for implementing it can be very debatable. Communicate the logic behind the implementation strategy. Involve people as much as possible in implementation planning. Be clear about any fundamental values of the implementation that explain its steps such as, "Everyone affects quality so everyone will be trained."

"I'm cynical about this place really changing."

In other words, I'm cynical about other people around here, particularly senior people, really changing. Based on what I've seen, I don't think this change will really last. I believe that when the rubber meets the road, the company isn't really committed. Let's see them do it first — I'll wait and see.

The leaders have to really do it — over and over again. A message of change has to be repeated again and again to be "heard" by the majority of the organization. Natasha Josefowitz, in *Paths To Power,* observes wryly, "A behavior has to be repeated seventeen times before it becomes believable to others!"

"I'm afraid I'm not going to do well in this."

In other words, I'm afraid of losing face, losing power, or losing my job. When communicating about change, take a page from the Federal Express approach to communication. Federal Express assumes that every associate has three questions all the time:

Clarity: "What do you expect of me?"

Reward: "What's in it for me?"

Justice: "Where do I go with a problem?"

Clear answers to these questions are the best responses to fears.

John Lawrie, in the *Training & Development* article "The ABC's of Change," has these observations about our human reactions to change:

1. People are funny. We view change that we initiate as needed and valuable. We resist change that is forced on us, no matter what the change is.

2. We need predictability — physical, psychological, and social. It is part of our basic need for security.

3. We also need variety, creative outlets, and breaks in routine.

4. Therefore, we must bring about change without threatening security.

Lawrie has the following suggestions:

• Provide as much lead time as possible.

• Allow people to participate in creating and installing the change.

• Expect resistance.

• Do not expect a uniform rate of change.

• Identify innovative groups and use them as pilots.

• Communicate the expected benefits of the change.

• Reward change.

Responding To Learned Resistance

Learned resistance to change often occurs when change efforts reach a plateau. On a plateau, the pace of change stalls and feelings of doubt about the organization's ability to change appear. Your change effort may be plateauing if you observe some of these symptoms:

- Despite lots of effort, many teams and lots of dollars, overall performance of the organization has not improved.
- It is hard to describe, with facts, how the process is going. Only anecdotal reports are available. If activity data are tracked, it is hard to link the activities to organizational results.
- People refer to the change effort in the past tense.
- Customers cannot tell you what the change effort means for them.
- The initiative has not produced noticeable changes in the behavior and practices of the leaders.
- New employees do not experience a different culture than the one described by veteran employees.

Reasons For Learned Resistance

There are many reasons for the plateauing effect. One is simply that it is far easier to *want* to change than to actually change. Also, we tend to be better at spotting the need for change in others — other people, other divisions, other companies — than at changing ourselves. Other reasons include:

- Underestimating the work
- Focusing primarily on training
- Low or vague expectations for the change
- Too much patience
- Inadequate leadership
- Disconnection from strategy

Underestimating The Work

The work and resources required in a change effort are not well understood at the outset. Change efforts often begin with a flurry of energy that is long on aspiration and short on implementation specifics. Certainly no one would think of starting construction on a skyscraper without a comprehensive plan, but this sometimes happens with organizational change. It's O.K. to call it a journey as long as you supply maps.

In addition, because there is no database for assessing the magnitude of the change task, the resources needed are often underestimated. In some efforts, one mid-level person may be assigned to "implement quality" in a 10,000-person organization! The more specific the implementation plan, the more realistic the estimate of resources can be.

Focusing Primarily On Training

Implementing a change requires learning a new set of skills and tools. Training is tangible and can be scheduled and coordinated. Training, however, assures little or no change in behavior. Without a plan to support on-the-job applications of newly learned practices, change doesn't occur. An organizational change effort is not soley a training effort.

Low Or Vague Expectations For The Change

If performance improvement goals are not specifically defined and new cultural characteristics are not envisioned, there is inadequate fuel in the engine of change. Motorola fueled its change effort with aggressive goals on the order of tenfold improvements in cycle time and defects.

Too Much Patience

Although implementing organizational change successfully may take three-to-five years, there is no time to lose. Some increment of change must take place daily. Otherwise, the plan will continually stretch into the seemingly unreachable future. An unwritten law (until now!) is that if nothing really changes in nine months, the change effort loses its credibility.

Leadership Is Inadequate

Leaders who make the initial speech and then return to "more important" tasks destine their efforts to failure. Leaders must be out in front, living the new culture.

Disconnection From Strategy

If a change effort is planned as an initiative unto itself, it will suffer from disconnection. Failure to connect the change effort to the overall strategy and annual plans of the business is a common mistake.

Responding To Learned Resistance To Change

The best way to respond to learned resistance is to assess and modify the change effort. Change efforts are actually quite resilient. With a renewed focus, a change effort can become what it was originally intended to be. Some effective strategies are the following.

Conduct A Thorough Self Assessment

Develop a survey based on your organizational principles and conduct it throughout the company. The results of the survey will tell how well the company is living its philosophy, as well as provide areas of focus and an impetus for change. Honest feedback from associates provides a clear picture of reality. Basing a survey on your statement of principles can give that document a renewed vigor.

Set Ambitious Goals And Expect Results

Translate the mission and vision of the organization into quantifiable performance improvement targets. These "mission measures" can be used to judge progress and put a dose of reality into lofty language. Such measures prevent the vision from becoming a mirage and the mission from turning to mush.

Plan, And Plan To Replan

Develop a comprehensive plan. One of our clients has taken the task of planning for change to a highly refined level. One-year and three-year visions are broken into 90- and 180-day plans with specific benchmarks. Within a 90-day period, it is clear whether the plan is on-track or has fallen behind. In either case, the next 90-day plan is built based on progress-to-date.

Change The Systems

Signal the rebirth of your effort by changing some of the systems that support the old culture. For example, performance evaluation systems can be based 50% on team performance and 50% on individual performance. Such changes make the new culture real today.

Test Against External Criteria

Use the criteria from the Malcolm Baldrige National Quality Award to assess the scope of your overall effort. ISO 9000 can also provide an external reference point. These criteria broaden the base of your change effort and help address the business as a system.

Consultant Resistance

Consultants resist just as clients do. Consultants sometimes resist reporting, giving feedback, contacting, contracting, confronting, or giving advice.

Reasons For Consultant Resistance

Consultants resist and seek comfort in the familiar for the following reasons.

Fatigue

As Vince Lombardi observed, "Fatigue makes cowards of us all." A consultant, exhausted after a long day of training and coaching, bumps into the top client in the elevator. The top clients asks, "How's it going?" The consultant, too tired for another interaction and eager for a kind word, says, "Fine." The top client says, "How are the troops reacting?" The consultant says something vague like, "They had some initial reservations, but they're coming along." That's it. An opportunity has been lost for genuine interaction. The consultant has started to pretend that everything's O.K.

Several issues are relevant here. The consultant should always have an "elevator speech" ready. An "elevator speech" is a two-minute description (the length of an elevator ride) of what's you're doing, why it's important, how it's going, and what the top client needs to know or do. An example would be:

"We're halfway through our process analysis of the order-to-cash process. We expect to be able to reduce the cycle time of the process by at least one-half. We have already come up with a lot of ideas for radically improving the process. The best part about the effort is the cross-functional communication among the members of the team. The toughest part will be the sense of turf among those who operate the process today. We may need your help there."

Realize that a senior manager looks across the horizon of strategies, projects, and action plans thinking, "That one's O.K....that one needs some attention...that's going well...that one's off to a good start...that one's about to go down the tubes." A chance meeting or casual conversation may be the moment to make the change effort observable on that horizon. Realize also that senior managers hear all the time that everything's going O.K. and are skeptical that it's true. Genuine conversation distinguishes you.

A consultant must maintain enough energy to provide deliverables *and* manage relationships. A consultant who is too busy to manage client relationships is letting consulting become harder than it has to be.

Bad Past Experiences

Sooner or later, every consultant gets read the riot act, gets the cold shoulder, or otherwise gets treated badly. It happens to everyone (one of our colleagues was spit upon by a key stakeholder during the implementation of a total quality process). Being a consultant is a high-risk endeavor and sometimes, rightfully or not, a top client says, "This isn't working and it's your fault," or, "We don't have time for this anymore." You may not be sure what happened, but whatever happened feels bad and feels like it was your fault. These experiences can lead a consultant to be gun-shy, avoiding senior managers, resisting confrontational situations, and focusing only on champions, stars, and favorite activities.

Unsure About Observations Or Advice

Is my advice correct? Did I really see that? If I'm the only one to notice that, am I crazy? Our advice is often "soft" advice. We are asking our clients to ask questions, allow decision making, give feedback, share recognition, and state a vision. We may fear that our advice will not be received as well as "hard" advice to invest capital, develop a new product, or change marketing strategies.

Unsure About Reactions

How will the client react to my comments? Will the client become angry? Will the client stop the project or reject me as the consultant? Will the client attribute problems to my lack of skills? Will it seem like I oversold the approach? Will I have to confront the client on his or her own shortcomings?

Unsure About The Approach

Will the approach I'm advocating really produce the result that the client is looking for? Will these interventions really help the organization? Will implementing this approach really help the client be successful? Is this approach strong enough medicine?

Lack Of Experience

How do senior managers talk? What do they think about? A consultant may be in the habit of being deferential. It's easy to stay with the familiar — I know how to teach a class, but I'm not sure I know how to give a senior manager feedback, so I think I'll focus on teaching the class.

Responding To Your Own Resistance

Here are some ways for consultants to handle their own resistance.

Controlling Your Thoughts And Emotions

As Peter Block has pointed out in *Flawless Consulting,* all consultants have concerns about three issues: credibility, competence, and credit. Our concern about credibility is, "Do they take me seriously as a consultant?" Our concern about competence is, "Am I good enough to provide the desired deliverables?" Our concern about credit is, "Am I going to get credit for my contribution, or is the client going to take all the credit?"

Not surprising, the client usually has the same concerns: "Is the consultant going to take me seriously in my role?" "Is the consultant going to consider me competent?" "Am I going to get credit or is the consultant going to take all the credit?" As consultants, we must avoid projecting our concerns onto the client. In other words, a consultant who feels that he or she is not being taken seriously is likely to question the credibility of the client. A consultant who is anxious about being good enough is likely to view the client as incompetent. A consultant who is concerned about credit is not likely to give credit to the client.

As a consultant, you can "borrow" credibility by aligning yourself with the approach you are implementing. For example, you might say, "The total quality approach would say that the cost of quality is about 25% of total revenue," or "The reengineering school of thought would ask whether that work should be done at all." Furthermore, a consultant should not hide his or her credentials. If you have completed special training, visited other companies, attended organizational improvement conferences, or talked to other internal or external consultants, you should let your clients know this. Your clients don't have to see you as a nationally-known guru, but they should realize that you are more knowledgeable in these areas than many others in the organization.

With regard to your competence, be both aggressive and self-aware. You can probably perform more consulting services than you may think, and you should be courageous about trying new things. On the other hand, there is no reason to expect yourself to provide every service. Use other internal consultants and external consultants when needed.

With regard to credit, you should have determined "what's a good job" as well as your roles and responsibilities with the client during contracting. If that has occurred, you have done what you can to ensure that you receive fair recognition. You can then ignore all other issues of credit.

Mental Toughness

James E. Loehr, in *Toughness Training for Life*, offers key advice about tough thinking that is very relevant to consultants.

Start thinking more responsively. Develop a keen mental awareness of negative emotional states such as depression, assumption of defeat, helplessness, and the like. Don't just accept them and muddle through. Investigate why you feel that way, devise a solution, and put it into effect.

Start thinking more flexibly. Don't say or think you hate something, someone, or some group of people. Don't say or think you can't do something. Don't think "never" as in, "I never get any breaks," or "I'll never make it."

Start thinking more resiliently. Think thoughts like, "I can handle this," "I've been through worse things than this," "This is not too much for me," and "I bounce back quickly."

Start thinking more energetically and more humorously. Think fun. Think or say, "I love this," and "Is this great or what?" In almost every situation, being able to laugh puts you in emotional control. Laughing under pressure is a learnable skill. For example, how many consultants does it take to screw in a lightbulb?

Answer #1: I don't know. How many consultants do *you* think it takes? Tell more about that.

Answer #2: I don't know, but we could form a study team.

Answer #3: Three. One to unscrew it, one to listen carefully, and one to observe group interactions.

You get the idea.

View mistakes differently. Ask yourself, "What could I, or should I, have done differently? What can I learn from this? What can I take away from this that will help me in the future?" Then say, "It's over. I'm letting it go. It's history. I'm leaving the past behind. It's time to move on."

Summary

In this chapter, we have discussed how to help someone face change, how to respond to initial and learned resistance, and how to spot and handle our own resistance as consultants.

Keeney Hupp
1 May '95

References

Chapter 1

Barker, Joel Arthur. *Future Edge: Discovering the New Paradigms of Success.* New York: Morrow, 1992.

Bridges, William. *Transitions: Making Sense of Life's Changes.* Reading, Massachusetts: Addison-Wesley, 1980.

Bridges, William. *Managing Transitions: Making the Most of Change.* Reading, Massachusetts: Addison-Wesley, 1991.

Carkhuff, Robert R. *The Art Of Helping VI.* Amherst, Massachusetts: Human Resource Development Press, 1987.

Conner, Daryl R. *Managing At The Speed Of Change: How Resilient Managers Succeed and Prosper Where Others Fail.* New York: Villard Books, 1993.

Hammer, Michael, and James Champy. *Reengineering the Corporation: A Manifesto for Business Revolution.* New York: Harper Business, 1993.

Kübler-Ross, Elisabeth. *On Death and Dying.* 1969.

Kulik, James A., Peter Jaksa, and Chen-Lin C. Kulik. "Component Analysis of Personalized Instruction." *The Journal of Personalized Instruction,* Volume 3, Number 1, Spring 1978, pp. 2-14.

Senge, Peter M. *The Fifth Discipline: The Art & Practice of the Learning Organization.* New York: Doubleday Currency, 1990.

Tichy, Noel M., and Mary Anne Devanna. *The Transformational Leader.* New York: John Wiley & Sons, 1986, 1990.

Tichy, Noel M., and Stratford Sherman. *Control Your Destiny Or Someone*

Else Will. New York: Currency Doubleday, 1993.

Toynbee, Arnold J. *A Study of History.* New York: Oxford University Press/ Dell Publishing, 1946.

Chapter 2

Association for Quality and Participation, The. *Voices From The Field.* Published Research. Cincinnati, Ohio: The Association for Quality and Participation, 1993.

Block, Peter. *Flawless Consulting: A Guide To Getting Your Expertise Used.* San Diego: University Associates, Inc., 1981.

Chapter 3

Alessandra, Tony, and Phil Hunsaker. *Communicating At Work.* New York: Simon & Schuster, 1993.

Block, Peter. *Flawless Consulting: A Guide To Getting Your Expertise Used.* San Diego: University Associates, Inc., 1981.

Fisher, Roger, and William Ury. *Getting To Yes: Negotiating Agreement Without Giving In.* New York: Bantam Books, 1981.

Lynch, Robert F., and Thomas J. Werner. *Continuous Improvement: Teams & Tools.* Milwaukee, Wisconsin: ASQC/Quality Press, 1992.

Mager, Robert, and Peter Pipe. *Analyzing Performance Problems, or You Really Oughta Wanna.* Belmont, California: Fearon, 1970.

Peters, Thomas J., and Robert H. Waterman. *In Search of Excellence: Lessons from America's Best-Run Companies.* New York: Warner Books, 1982.

Shapiro, Benson P., V. K. Rangan, and J. J. Sviokla. "Staple Yourself to an

Invoice." *Harvard Business Review*, July-August 1992.

Tichy, Noel M., and Stratford Sherman. *Control Your Destiny Or Someone Else Will*. New York: Currency Doubleday, 1993.

Tichy, Noel M. "Revolutionize Your Company." *Fortune,* December 13, 1993, pp. 114-118.

Ury, William. *Getting Past No: Negotiating Your Way From Confrontation To Cooperation*. New York: Bantam Books, 1991.

Chapter 4

Imai, Masaaki. *Kaizen: The Key to Japan's Competitive Success*. New York: Random House, 1986..

Garvin, David. "Competing on the Eight Dimensions of Quality." *Harvard Business Review,* 1987.

Lynch, Robert F., and Thomas J. Werner. *Continuous Improvement: Teams & Tools*. Milwaukee, Wisconsin: ASQC/Quality Press, 1992.

Zemke, Ron, with Dick Schaaf. *The Service Edge: 101 Companies That Profit from Customer Care*. New York: Plume, 1989.

Chapter 5

Lynch, Robert F., and Thomas J. Werner. *Continuous Improvement: Teams & Tools*. Milwaukee, Wisconsin: ASQC/Quality Press, 1992.

Chapter 7

Lynch, Robert F., and Thomas J. Werner. *Continuous Improvement: Teams & Tools*. Milwaukee, Wisconsin: ASQC/Quality Press, 1992.

Lynch, Robert F., and Thomas J. Werner. *Reengineering Business Processes and People Systems*. Atlanta, Georgia: QualTeam, 1994.

Chapter 9

AMA Management Briefing. *Blueprints for Service Quality: The Federal Express Approach*. New York: American Management Association, 1991.

Block, Peter. *Flawless Consulting: A Guide To Getting Your Expertise Used*. San Diego: University Associates, Inc., 1981.

Bridges, William. *Managing Transitions: Making the Most of Change*. Reading, Massachusetts: Addison-Wesley, 1991.

Carkhuff, Robert R. *The Art Of Helping VI*. Amherst, Massachusetts: Human Resource Development Press, 1987.

Conner, Daryl R. *Managing At The Speed Of Change: How Resilient Managers Succeed and Prosper Where Others Fail*. New York: Villard Books, 1993.

Josefowitz, Natasha. *Paths To Power*. Reading, Massachusetts: Addison-Wesley, 1980.

Lawrie, John. "The ABCs of Change Management." *Training & Development Journal*, March 1990, Volume 44, Number 3, pp. 87-89.

Loehr, James E. *Toughness Training For Life*. New York: Dutton, 1993.

Tichy, Noel M., and Mary Anne Devanna. *The Transformational Leader*. New York: John Wiley & Sons, 1986, 1990.